Advance Praise for *For Love of Animals*

♦ ♦ ♦

"*For Love of Animals* is a compelling piece of popular Catholic moral theology that advocates for profound change in western and Christian moral attitudes and practices in relation to non-human animals. Camosy draws deftly on Scripture and Catholic moral tradition especially, while also listening respectfully to secular thinkers such as Peter Singer. These voices demanding that non-human animals be included in our moral community are then contrasted with the grotesque mistreatment of animals in our factory farms, medical research, and some hunting practices. After a while, the author has us checkmated—if we Christians (and others) would live in a manner consistent with our own most cherished principles, it appears highly doubtful that we can any longer kill animals for fun, research, or food. This book is the most compelling and accessible presentation of our relationship to our non-human animal neighbors that I have ever seen."

—Dr. David P. Gushee, Distinguished University Professor of
Christian Ethics and Director, Center for Theology
and Public Life, Mercer University

♦ ♦ ♦

"In a brisk, friendly, and graceful style, Charles Camosy invites us to think clearly about the moral problem of cruelty to animals—and about the moral opportunity it presents. He writes in the tradition of C.S. Lewis, G.K. Chesterton, and other great Christian minds who abhorred cruelty in any form, and through reasoned moral judgment advocated for consistent and merciful conduct in our dealings with other creatures. As in the best Christian writing, there's an integrity and simplicity to the argument that Camosy offers, and the most persuasive influence can be the kind hearted example of the author himself."

—Matthew Scully, author of *Dominion*
and former presidential speechwriter

FOR LOVE OF ANIMALS

Charles Camosy

• • •

FOR LOVE
OF
ANIMALS

Christian Ethics,
Consistent Action

Franciscan
MEDIA
Cincinnati, Ohio

Cover and book design by Mark Sullivan
Cover/title page image © Eric Gevaert | Fotolia
Back cover image © dundanim | Fotolia

LIBRARY OF CONGRESS CATALOGING-IN-PUBLICATION DATA
Camosy, Charles Christopher.
For love of animals : Christian ethics, consistent action / Charles Camosy.
pages cm
Summary: "For Love of Animals is an honest and thoughtful look at our responsibility as Christians with respect to animals. Many Christians misunderstand both history and their own tradition in thinking about animals. They are joined by prominent secular thinkers who blame Christianity for the Western world's failure to seriously consider the moral status of animals. This book explains how traditional Christian ideas and principles—like nonviolence, concern for the vulnerable, respect for life, stewardship of God's creation, and rejection of consumerism—require us to treat animals morally"— Provided by publisher.
ISBN 978-1-61636-662-9 (pbk.)
1. Animals—Religious aspects—Christianity. 2. Animal welfare—Religious aspects—Christianity. 3. Christian ethics. I. Title.
BT746.C35 2013
241'.693—dc23
2013025776

ISBN 978-1-61636-662-9

Published by Franciscan Media
28 W. Liberty St.
Cincinnati, OH 45202
www.FranciscanMedia.org

Printed in the United States of America.
Printed on acid-free paper.
13 14 15 16 17 5 4 3 2 1

for Paulyn Joy
wife and treasured partner in all things,
including concern for animals

CONTENTS

◆ ◆ ◆

ACKNOWLEDGMENTS

◆ ◆ ◆

As with all book projects, the final result comes from a community of people rather than a single person.

I am so grateful for Franciscan Media's generous support for this project. And in particular I want to highlight acquisitions editor Alicia von Stamwitz for her vision and energy, without which this book simply would not have been possible. I also want to thank Beth Haile, Francesca Battista, and Karen Allanach for reading through drafts of the manuscript and offering very helpful feedback.

I must also acknowledge my undergraduate and graduate students at Fordham University. If there are any insights worth exploring in this book, chances are they came directly from the many dozens of exchanges I've been fortunate enough to have about animals in Fordham seminar rooms. These exchanges were almost always at a very high level, but they also directly connected to real-life practices and experiences.

It is particularly important for me to highlight some people who have helped shape my attitudes and practices with respect to animals: Mom and Dad, Anne Hugunin, Tony Biehn, Clancy Camosy, Katie Ball-Boruff, Alisha Mack, and Wes Foreman. And still others have helped foster concern for animals specifically in a religious context: John Berkman, David Clough, Sue Kopp, Andy Alexis-Baker, Christine Gutleben, Grace Kao, and Aaron Gross.

Sincere thanks to each of you.

FOREWORD

· ◆ ·

EVERY ONCE IN A WHILE, a book comes along that does something few books ever do, which is to change something fundamental about the way you live your life. For some people reading these words, theologian Charles Camosy's *For Love of Animals* will be that book.

And for good reason: its subject—the rights and wrongs of our modern treatment of animals, especially (though not only) mammals, and especially (though not only) the creatures of factory farms—is simultaneously morally urgent and widely ignored by many people, including and inexplicably by many well-meaning but hitherto under-informed Christians.

Dr. Camosy has now remedied that defect with this lively, thoughtful, and original book. It ranges widely but with a teacherly touch over subjects as diverse as the history of Christian vegetarianism; papal and other pronouncements about creation; the development of Christian theology concerning nonhuman persons, such as angels; the morality of dogfighting; the relevance of laws against child labor; the question of pets; the truth about factory farming; and much more. Throughout, the author convinces the reader both that our culture's treatment of defenseless creatures is morally indefensible much of the time; and also that "those of us who follow Jesus Christ," in particular, "should give animals special moral consideration and attention."

For Love of Animals applies the specific lens of Catholic teaching about social justice, pointing out among other details that the *Catechism of the Catholic Church* itself says that animals are *owed* moral treatment (2415–2418; none of these specifically says "owed moral treatment"). Its author is surely right to attribute the horrors of factory farming, in particular, to an ethic of feckless consumption according to which more is better, all the time.

It is rampant and unexamined Western consumerism, more than anything else, that "disconnects[s] us from the process by which pig meat gets on our plate." I would add to that analysis the friendly amendment that this same consumerism encourages the formation of a habit that is suspect wherever and whenever it appears, but that chronically gets a pass where animals are involved: that is, a practiced desire to remain ignorant of those things about which we wish not to know.

Of course reasonable and good people will disagree about some of what's discussed in these pages. Moreover, as the author emphasizes, fundamental cultural change takes time—lots of it. But surely every reader, Christian or otherwise, can agree, upon reading this book, that in the matter of animals, lines ought to be drawn and distinctions ought to be made that aren't currently part of our Western moral topography—and need to be.

The map toward a better kind of stewardship has many and varied roads, some of them personal. Like the author, I also gave up eating mammals and birds some time back after decades of itinerant vegetarianism; and for me, too, this was a gradual and parallel effort toward becoming "more authentically and consistently pro-life," as he puts it in describing his own path.

In my own case, as it turned out, that change had less to do with philosophical questions about species-ism than with more visceral things. In particular, I simply could not get around a question raised vividly in Matthew Scully's seminal 2002 book *Dominion: The Power of Man, the Suffering of Animals, and the Call to Mercy:* If I was unwilling to kill these creatures with my own bare hands (as I surely was, and am), then by what right or moral standard could I possibly delegate the brutal act of killing to others—especially to those poorer and darker and more desperate "others" who man America's squealing slaughterhouses and shovel out its reeking chicken factories?

It took a few years and plenty of other questions, but ultimately *Dominion* decisively affected my life; and the same will be true for other people upon reading *For Love of Animals*.

In addition to being merciful, the book is also a mercifully good read. It can and should be paged with profit by anyone from high school age on up. Readers seeking a thoughtful presentation to family or friends of their own reasons for abstaining from meat will find in it an especially useful primer, and readers who are nowhere near convinced will nonetheless find that it opens their eyes.

It would be gratifying if the book were also to start a serious discussion in Christian religious quarters. One wonders, for example, whether vegetarianism for some believers might be a unique "sign of contradiction" in its own right—particularly in a time of relative plenty marked by rampant consumerism, and particularly given what Pope John Paul II decried as an accompanying "culture of death." Wanton cruelty to animals, of the sort that is now pitiably routine, is arguably part and parcel of that same culture, and it further deadens the general moral sense at a time when it's arguably needed most.

As a vegetarian named Leo Tolstoy once put it, in a powerful 1909 essay that he wrote about a slaughterhouse: "[W]e cannot pretend that we do not know this. We are not ostriches, and cannot believe that if we refuse to look at what we do not wish to see, it will not exist."

One also wonders after reading this book when, if ever, pro-life and pro-animal advocates will figure out how much they have in common and make common cause. To observe as much is hardly to posit moral equivalence. It's rather to make the point that those who labor to protect unborn human life have more in common with many animal sympathizers than either side has yet understood, as some people reading these pages are about to find out. Similarly, readers might note the almost preternatural serendipity of this book's appearance during the pontificate of a pope named Francis I, named for the greatest animal lover of all time— one more sign suggesting that the moment for a fair hearing of Camosy's argument is ripe.

In sum, whether you are a Catholic or an atheist, liberal or conservative, progressive or traditionalist, or somewhere in between all those distinctions, the pages ahead will give you much to think about. And you won't be alone. Every year, more Western men and women are being driven to understand that solicitude for human animals and solicitude for other animals are not mutually exclusive expenditures of moral energy. More and more can now agree that stewardship is a call to clemency and mercy, not to ruthless exploitation; and that all life, including animal life, is too precious to be cavalierly and cruelly and routinely trashed.

The community of people now struggling to understand as much, and to do right by creatures both great and small, is in the process of constructing a wholly new big tent. Thanks to Camosy's welcome contribution, it just got noticeably bigger.

Mary Eberstadt
Senior fellow with the Ethics and Public Policy Center,
Washington DC
August 2013

CHAPTER ONE

JUSTICE FOR ANIMALS?

IF YOU ARE PRO-LIFE, chances are you are familiar with the
following story. While in the middle of a somewhat awkward
discussion with a person you don't know very well, somehow
the conversation drifts toward the topic of abortion. After a
brief exchange of ideas, this person discovers your pro-life position and, despite the fact that you have attacked neither him nor
his pro-choice position, he reacts defensively. He spends several
minutes aggressively offering reasons why the position you hold
is mistaken. Merely encountering a pro-life position on abortion
is often enough to provoke this kind of strong reaction from those
who disagree.

About ten years ago I became convinced that, if I wanted to
be authentically and consistently pro-life, I should give up eating
meat. Those of us who do not eat meat have probably found
ourselves in the following situation. You are eating a community
meal with someone who doesn't know your dietary restrictions.
Perhaps in the context of politely passing on the meat when it is
offered to you, your conversation partner discovers that you think
eating meat is morally wrong and reacts defensively. Perhaps
she offers several detailed reasons why she thinks eating meat

is justified. Interestingly, some of the most aggressive reactions I've encountered in this kind of situation have come from fellow Christians.

Beyond the fact that both points of view provoke these kinds of reactions (we will explore why they do below), do they have anything else in common? I would argue that both are stances in defense of justice. The most important position that many pro-lifers defend—that our prenatal children deserve equal protection of the law—is a claim about justice for these children. But justice is a slippery concept that people can understand in very different ways. For instance, social justice is at once at the heart of what many liberals believe an ethical society requires, while for many conservatives this is just code for growing government to serve a political agenda.

Justice is indeed a complicated topic. Dozens and dozens of books try to explain what it is, and some of them were written several centuries before Jesus was born. Obviously I cannot dive into this kind of complexity here (please see some of the suggested reading at the end of each chapter if you are interested in learning more), but the following definition captures much of what the best thinkers have said about the topic:

DOING JUSTICE MEANS BEING CONSISTENT
AND IMPARTIAL IN GIVING INDIVIDUALS AND
GROUPS WHAT THEY ARE OWED.

Given this definition, we can think about multiple kinds of injustice. Someone could be inconsistent in applying one's principles—perhaps especially in situations where it goes against that person's self-interest or political commitments to be consistent. For instance, some people inconsistently (and therefore unjustly) ignore the dignity of prenatal children because it would force them to confront uncomfortable questions about their position on abortion—even when they generally favor nonviolence and protection of vulnerable populations in other situations.

Injustice could also involve undue partiality for certain people over others. For instance, some show partial (and therefore unjust) concern for their family members when they spend tens of thousands of dollars on unnecessary luxuries like high-end cars, exotic vacations, designer clothes, jewelry, and so on—all while many hundreds of thousands of innocent children die of easily treatable diseases.

A serious kind of injustice takes place when we refuse to recognize certain individuals or groups as the kinds of beings to which we owe moral behavior. For instance, for much of our history both women and peoples of color were put into the "other" category with the result that those in power didn't have to think much about what they were owed. These communities were sometimes explicitly understood to be property, to be used as those in power saw fit. Overwhelming majorities of us now recognize this as unjust and rightly call these ideas racist and sexist. But because most Western cultures labeled women and peoples of color as "other"—to whom little or nothing is owed—they did not recognize it as such.

Perhaps one reason why questions of justice are often so difficult to discuss—and provoke such strong reactions—is that a genuine concern for justice means that we must risk rethinking our familiar and comfortable ways of seeing the world. We are challenged not only to rethink our views and politics, but also our behavior. Nineteenth-century white men discussing the right to vote or slavery were sometimes provoked to anger by those who pushed for just treatment of women and African Americans. Why? Because giving these populations what they were owed demanded that those with power not only change their views, but also that they change their behavior and give up some of their power. Indeed, it demanded that a whole culture change its unjust ways. Justice for our prenatal children—and, as I mean to show throughout this book, for animals as well—demands nothing less.

A Christian Understanding of Justice

Now, a generic concept of justice has mostly uncontroversial support from both explicitly religious and secular people. But once we get into the nitty-gritty specifics of justice and how it plays out with a variety of issues and topics, things get more complicated and controversial. I'm writing this book as a Catholic Christian ethicist, and my tradition has a very particular understanding of justice, developed over many centuries. At its foundation is the biblical account of the life of Jesus: a man who lived with primary concern for the powerless "others" on the margins on the community: the poor, the sick, the stranger, the prisoner, the immigrant, the child. Catholic social doctrine therefore claims that Christians must have a "preferential option" for these vulnerable populations. A Christian conception of justice will be different from the first definition given above because it is partial in that it favors those on the margins over those in power.

Another essential aspect of Jesus's life was his emphasis on peace, and any Christian concept of justice inspired by Jesus, the Prince of Peace must be suspicious of violence. Indeed, the *Compendium of the Social Doctrine of the Church* teaches that injustice itself—and unjust laws, in particular—is violence. Consider laws that permit exploitive child labor. Such laws, according to Catholic social teaching, are "a kind of violence that is less obvious than others but it is not for this reason any less terrible." This kind of structural or social violence, then, must also be a focus of a Christian understanding of justice.

It is tempting to think of peacefulness as merely the passive refusal to be violent—especially when we live in a culture of freedom and autonomy that emphasizes the duty to leave others alone. But if it is truly Christian peacefulness, inspired by a person who claims that love should be the source of our ultimate concern, it must involve loving action or charity. Far from mere giving, Christian charity requires that we imitate Jesus's active loving-kindness for all. This fulfills Jesus's central command to love our neighbor as ourselves. Especially if that neighbor is in need, Christianity requires that we come to his or her aid and actively seek justice. This kind of active work for justice (remember, with a preference for the most vulnerable) is so important that, should we fail to perform it, Jesus tells us that we risk cutting ourselves off from God altogether:

> Then he will say to those at his left hand, "You that are accursed, depart from me into the eternal fire prepared for the devil and his angels; for I was hungry and you gave me no food, I was thirsty and you gave me nothing to drink, I was a stranger and you did not welcome me, naked and you did not give me clothing, sick and in prison and you did not visit me." (Matthew 25:41–43)

Finally, a Christian conception of justice, though it is grounded in the Bible and the historical wisdom of the Church, must engage the real world. It must be particularly aware of forces that promote injustice in our own time and context. The forces of violence have threatened justice throughout human history, and continue to do so, but we have two important threats that have arisen in the last few decades: (1) an overemphasis on "privacy" and "freedom," and (2) a detached and overwhelming drive to consume. Spurred by American politics, too many of us focus first on the freedom of the individual to do as she pleases. This not only tempts us to avoid considering how our own behavior contributes to injustice, but it also keeps us from actively seeking justice for vulnerable people at the level of our culture or society. After all, if our active love for the vulnerable spurs us to try to change laws to protect them from injustice, then we are working to constrain the freedom and choice of those who are violently dominating them. And in a related idea, we must also judge this behavior as fundamentally unjust—a difficult thing to do in a culture which, because of its overwhelming focus on freedom and choice, hesitates to judge behavior at all.

But if there is a runner-up to freedom as the value our secular political culture holds most dear, it is consumerism. The American dream is not about love, happiness, faith, or family, but rather about having consumed enough to live in a large home with a substantial yard, own two or three cars, take expensive vacations, and generally be as independent from others as possible. When this goal trumps a concern for justice (as it often does), many vulnerable people get hurt. In an effort to consume products at the cheapest possible prices, for instance, the overwhelming majority of us are distanced from the source of the things we buy. Most of us have no idea where our clothes, food, and other everyday items come from or how they get to us. Indeed, our distance has reached a new level when we can buy products with the click of a smart phone and have them almost magically show up at our door—sometimes only hours later. We have no idea how our choices to consume this way contribute to, say, exploitation of workers (both locally and overseas), degradation of our world's ecology, the affordability of products for people in developing countries, and—yes—the cruel treatment of animals. When consumerism dominates our culture as it does today, the injustice done to vulnerable populations becomes virtually invisible.

So, given what we just considered, how should we describe a Christian conception of justice? Let's use the framework from the first definition, but change it with respect to the Christian concerns discussed above. I think we get something like this:

"CHRISTIAN JUSTICE MEANS CONSISTENTLY AND ACTIVELY WORKING TO SEE THAT INDIVIDUALS AND GROUPS—ESPECIALLY VULNERABLE POPULATION ON THE MARGINS—ARE GIVEN WHAT THEY ARE OWED. IT WILL BE ESPECIALLY SKEPTICAL OF PRACTICES WHICH PROMOTE VIOLENCE, CONSUMERISM, AND AUTONOMY."

Justice for Animals?

It is easy to see how the Christian conception of justice could be applied to some of the populations already mentioned. When thinking about racism and African Americans, we can see how

Christians would be required to actively work to see that this vulnerable population—both as individuals and a group—receive just and equal treatment. African Americans were a marginalized population put into the "other" category. This was most evident when they became victims of the violent and consumerist-driven practice of slavery. The unjust laws of the Jim Crow era (and, just to name one of many examples, the predatory lending practices of banks today!) are a classic example of the violent social injustice mentioned above in the *Compendium*. Claims that others should not infringe on "their choice" to decide on how to treat African Americans in their states, schools, banks, and businesses have rightly been challenged. It is little wonder that Christians like Martin Luther King, Jr., led the way during the Civil Rights Movement using Christian Scripture and doctrine to support their arguments.

We can also see how this concept of justice could be applied to women and to prenatal children. Through most of history, women have been marginalized as somehow worth less than men. This "othering" opened the door to sexual and other kinds of violence, as well as unjust laws denying women opportunities such as the right to vote. Even today, women are the primary victims of sexual violence and of unjust policies in our culture—like the profit-driven practice of paying women less than men for the same work. And our prenatal children are one of the few populations today who are radically pushed to the margins as having virtually no significance at all—unless they are "wanted." More than fifty-five million of them have been victims of the violent and (largely) consumerist-driven practice of abortion since it became a constitutional right in the United States in 1973.

At this point you might be asking, "I thought this was a book about animals. Where are the animals?" Few people in our culture think about justice for animals, but that may be because few people think about what justice is in the first place. Before examining whether the concept of justice for animals makes sense, we needed to discuss justice apart from our discussion of animals. Given what we just learned about Christian justice, can we (rightly) talk about justice for animals? To begin to answer this question, let's get out of the heady and abstract discussion about justice and instead focus on a story—albeit a difficult one to hear.

Many readers will remember the rise and fall (and rise again) of National Football League quarterback Michael Vick. After starring at Virginia Tech (where he contended for the Heisman trophy) Vick was drafted number one overall by the Atlanta Falcons (the first African American quarterback to be so honored) and became one of the best, highest paid, and most popular players in the NFL. After six seasons, his time with the Falcons came to an end when he pled guilty to charges surrounding his financing of a dogfighting ring and admission that he hanged or drowned dogs who did not perform well. He was sentenced to two years in federal prison.

Once out of prison, Vick admitted his own wrongdoing and changed his ways. He started lobbying for more legal protection for dogs to shield them from violence. He even accepted an invitation to an eight-hour course on animal cruelty. (Interestingly, and important for the theme of this book, ESPN reported that Vick was "blown away" when he learned how much the Bible had to say about animals.) But the public had directed overwhelming anger at Vick when the news first broke and, despite his change of heart, this anger would fade only over time. Though he returned to the NFL to play for the Philadelphia Eagles, many believed his actions had been so awful that he should have been banned from the sport forever. Some thought he should have spent even more time in prison. *Fox News* analyst Tucker Carlson went even further, saying that Vick should have been "executed" for what he did to these dogs.

Where does this overwhelming anger come from? What precisely did Michael Vick do wrong? Some argue that he injured *himself*—after all, abusing dogs turns you into a cruel and violent person. But is this all he did? Would we say that Vick had injured himself if, instead of drowning dogs, he drowned several trees? Of course not. Then why is drowning a dog cruel and violent, but drowning a tree is not? The answer is in the harm that is done to the dog, a harm that is not done to the tree. When we ask, "What is it like for a tree to drown?" the answer is, "It isn't like anything because trees don't have experiences." When we ask, "What is it like for a dog to drown?" we respond, "It is horrifically awful." The wrongness of what Vick did consists primarily in the harm he did to those dogs. Whatever Vick did to himself, it was caused directly by the harm he did to the dogs.

OK, most agree that Vick harmed those dogs. But did Vick treat these dogs unjustly? Yes. Unlike trees, dogs are owed treatment from humans that is free from cruelty and violence. (Indeed, as we will see later in this book, the *Catechism of the Catholic Church* insists that animals are *owed* moral treatment.) Furthermore, Vick and others who run these dogfighting rings justify their behavior in ways that marginalize dogs and make them "other"—all in the name of a consumerist search for profit. Because the dogs are not members of the species *Homo sapiens*, Vick and others were able to ignore the dogs' claims to just treatment. We see similar reasoning in racism and sexism, don't we? Because African Americans are not white, slave owners and Jim Crow supporters (and others with power) put them into the "other" category and ignored their claims to just treatment. Because women are not men, powerful lawmakers put them into the "other" category and ignored their claims to just treatment. Michael Vick also engaged in "othering"—but instead of racism or sexism, he was guilty of *speciesism*.

What Is Speciesism?

This word sounds strange to our twenty-first–century ears, no doubt, and some dismiss this concept as yet another "ism" made up by out of touch academics in their ivory towers. But the words *racism* and *sexism* seemed equally strange at first to those who operated in a world where discrimination on the basis of race and sex was simply how the culture worked. Indeed, just as racism and sexism were virtually impossible to see at that time, speciesism goes unnoticed today. ("What water?" said the fish.) But as we go through this book and break down the ways in which our culture is fundamentally unjust to animals, the concept of speciesism will begin to sound more plausible. Indeed, given that this injustice comes to light for many millions each year, I predict that *speciesism* will not sound strange at all to the ears of the next generation.

There is another kind of unjust speciesism at work in the Michael Vick story. He received stinging and sustained criticism from many different kinds of people for what he did to dogs. But Vick did have defenders, and this post from *PhillyLawBlog* is a representative example:

11

You've simply swept the reality of factory farming under a rug because it's convenient. That steak you had for dinner? It was grown in the grocery store. Those delicious brats you ate while complaining about Michael Vick? They came from the freezer, not a pig that was castrated, tortured, and then killed. That fur coat? It came from the coat store, it wasn't stripped off an animal while it was still alive. But why are we talking about this anyway, it's such a drag...let's focus on a guy who was mean to dogs that resembled my pet! I love my pet!

Recall part of justice means being consistent when applying our principles. Why is there outrage about Vick's participation in animal cruelty, but not about the torturous existence of pigs in factory farms?

There are several explanations for this situation, but they are all speciesist. First, our culture differs from some others (especially some in Southeast Asia) in that dogs are primarily our pets and not our food. Many of us have such intense and positive social relationships with dogs such that we are emotionally affected when we think about their suffering. Pigs are at least as social and smart as dogs, but most of us buy and eat pig meat on a regular basis and thus participate in the cruel practices that factory farms use to bring us this food at a cheap price. Pigs are marginalized and "othered" so that we don't have to think about what kind of treatment we might owe them—especially as we bite into a piece of pepperoni pizza or bacon. Our consumerist social structures disconnect us from the process by which pig meat gets on our plate. There are ways to get protein that are more consistent with just treatment of animals, but most of us are not even thinking about them when we buy and eat our food. And on the rare occasions where we do think about them, we tell ourselves that they are too inconvenient or too costly. And sometimes, damn it, don't we just "need" to have a hot dog? At bottom, our choice to eat pigs and other kinds of animals often comes down to the fact that we have power and they do not.

It is simply inconsistent and therefore unjust to discriminate between dogs and pigs in this way. Perhaps we prefer one kind of species of animal over another because it is "cute" or because we find it easier to connect with its suffering. But if it is an injustice to treat dogs with cruel violence, then it is also an injustice to treat pigs with cruel violence. And our buying and eating pig meat is participation in this serious injustice. Given our understanding of justice as explained above, Christians must actively name and resist the violence and consumerism present in modern-day factory farming (something about which we will learn much more in chapter seven) both in our own personal lives and in our culture as a whole.

Some people, even if they are convinced that they should change their own practices to avoid speciesist and unjust treatment of animals, will nevertheless argue that they should not impose this belief on others. They might say, "It is wrong for me, but who am I to judge another's behavior?" But if we have a Christian conception of justice, this will not do. Recall that Christians are skeptical about appeals to autonomy and freedom when the issue at stake is one of justice. When we retreat into our own lives and do nothing more to change our social structures, vulnerable and marginalized populations get "othered"—especially when justice runs counter to the interests of the powerful. As Pope Francis said during the homily of his installation Mass on the Feast of St. Joseph, Christians have a moral duty to be protectors—not only for fellow human beings, but for all creation. If we are to stand for justice for animals we must do so not only in our own lives, but also by protecting them from the choices of others.

Some readers, especially if they have never really thought about these questions before, may find their heads spinning at this point. Even if you are generally convinced by the arguments presented so far, their implications may seem too overwhelming to consider. If that's the case, don't worry. The last three chapters of the book will walk us through the implications, step by step. Once they have had some time to sink in, all of this will seem less overwhelming. Living in just relationship with animals in our culture is not easy, but the challenges are not all that different from other challenges presented to us in other parts of our lives. Being a Christian isn't easy in our culture—period. This is especially true given that our culture is dominated by violence, consumerism, and autonomy.

Other readers might have different kinds of questions at this point, and they might go something like this. "This Camosy guy claims to be writing as a Christian, but all my life I've associated the 'animal rights crowd' with non-Christians and even enemies of the Church. Shouldn't we prioritize human life over animal life?" This important point of view is the subject of the next chapter.

QUESTIONS FOR DISCUSSION

1. What do you think of the concept of "speciesism"? Is it a legitimate concern for Christians? How is speciesism like racism and sexism? How might it be different?
2. Was Michael Vick wrong for doing what he did to dogs? Why? Did it involve an injustice to the dogs?

3. Is there any basis for concluding that cruelty to dogs is somehow morally different from cruelty to pigs? What might that basis be?

4. Some Christians believe that concern for justice for animals means less concern for justice for humans. Is this a legitimate worry?

Suggestions for Further Reading

Animal Sensibility and Inclusive Justice in *the Age of Bernard Shaw* by Rod Preece

Compendium of the Social Doctrine of the Church by the Pontifical Council for Justice and Peace

Deus Caritas Est by Pope Benedict XVI

Justice in Love by Nicholas Wolterstorff

Lost Dogs: Michael Vick's Dogs and the Tale of Their Rescue and Redemption by Jim Gorant

The Republic by Plato

A Theory of Justice by John Rawls

CHAPTER TWO

♦ ♦ ♦

CHRISTIANITY AND SPECIESISM

TRADITIONAL CHRISTIANS AND ATHEISTS DISAGREE, obviously, about many things. They disagree about whether God exists; they disagree about whether Christianity is a wholesome way of life; some disagree about how much human life is worth in comparison to animal life. But one thing about which they largely agree, unfortunately, is that Christianity is speciesist and responsible for the speciesism dominating our Western world. Christians speak publicly and often about the unique status of humans, alone made in the image of God, and about the dominion God has given human beings over animals to use them for food and clothing. But atheists concerned with animal rights often reject any privileged status for human beings, and will even rank the lives of some animals ahead of humans—especially prenatal and mentally damaged humans. Being an animal rights activist is frequently associated with atheism, while being a Christian is associated with being anti-animal rights. Both views, sadly, reinforce each other.

But it's even worse than this. There is a culture war going on between these two communities, and animals are used as pawns in this conflict. Many traditional Christians associate animal rights activism with a challenge to their fundamental beliefs about God and about the value of human life; their rejection of animal concerns becomes a way to defend their faith. Some in the secular community, by contrast, see Christian inconsistency with regard to animals as just another part of a religion they find primitive and foolish. The result? Traditional Christians cannot see any good coming from standing up for the dignity of animals, and atheists promoting animal rights see Christianity as a source of the problem rather than part of the solution.

This chapter will show that these two communities actually have a tremendous amount in common when it comes to how we should think about animals. Traditional Christianity is not fundamentally speciesist. And speciesism certainly had no need for Christianity in order to dominate human ideas and practices. But before making this case, let's examine the views of two famous thinkers who wish to blame traditional Christian thought for speciesist views in the Western world: Peter Singer and Lynn White, Jr.

Christianity as the Bad Guy, Part I: Peter Singer

Peter Singer is a chaired philosopher at Princeton University, and one could make the case that he is the most influential philosopher of our time. Someone trying to make this case would undoubtedly mention his book *Animal Liberation,* the groundbreaking work responsible for putting ethical concern for animals on the map. His career has gone beyond scholarship to more popular work to the extent that many animal activists see Peter Singer as the hero and founding father of their movement.

As we will see below, Singer lays much of the blame for how we got so off-track with animals at the feet of Christianity—so it is hardly surprising that so many animal activists simply follow suit. Furthermore, Singer explicitly and powerfully highlights the

Christian idea of the sanctity of human life as a major part of the problem. He even argues for a pro-choice stance (extending to infanticide) in cases of babies that are not yet (or never will be) rational and self-aware beings. With Singer as a primary public activist for animal rights, it is understandable that traditional Christians tend to associate the movement with hostility toward their point of view. But for all Singer's genius in bringing the cause of animals to the attention of the Western world (and it is genius, regardless of his fundamentally mistaken views on other matters), the story he tells about Christianity and the sanctity of human life has serious problems. Let's turn to that story now.

For Singer, what human animals have systematically done to nonhuman animals can be described as a kind of tyranny. In *Animal Liberation,* he says that in order to combat and overthrow tyranny we have to understand the ideas that sustain it. The ideas that sustain the view that animals are here to do with as we please appear most problematically in Christianity—which, he says, exported them all over the Western world. Christianity spread the idea that human life, and *only* human life, is sacred. It spread the idea that humans have dominion over other animals. It spread the idea that animals are not made in God's image. And so on.

Singer acknowledges that the Old Testament, or Hebrew Bible, has some good things to say about animals, but nothing in its overall vision challenges the tyrannical doctrine that humanity is the pinnacle of creation. The New Testament, he says, not only endorses this doctrine, but is completely silent on the issues of cruelty to animals or our duty to consider their interests. Singer is also unimpressed with the Church's postbiblical tradition.

Though he virtually ignores the Church Fathers, Singer claims that Christianity failed to temper the worst of Roman attitudes toward nonhuman animals. He also says that Christianity extinguished the spark of wider compassion for animals that had been kept alight by a small number of Greek and Roman thinkers. Indeed, he claims that we have to wait nearly sixteen hundred years until any Christian writer attacks cruelty to animals with any emphasis or detail.

Singer's conclusion is clear. To combat the tyranny directed against nonhuman animals, we must challenge and remove the Christian foundations of our Western attitudes and ideas. He says that few of us actually believe the theology that once justified these attitudes and ideas anyway, and so it should not be difficult to have what he calls a "second Copernican revolution." This time, instead of challenging and removing the theological idea that the earth is the center of the physical universe, we need to challenge and remove the theological idea that the human being is the center of the moral universe.

Responding to Singer

We will come back to the scriptural and doctrinal questions Singer raises, but we should begin by agreeing with him about the weakness of Christian sources on animals. As we will see in later chapters, Singer is mistaken about his sweepingly negative claims about Christian theology and animals, it is true that Christianity needs to do a better job of mining our resources on animals. But let's table these topics for the moment. Even if we acknowledge Christianity's limitations, does this mean Singer's "Christianity Is the Bad Guy" story is correct? Hardly. As British Christian ethicist David Clough reminded everyone at an important 2011 conference at the University of Oxford, Singer is badly mistaken about the history of speciesism.

No serious person could believe that, once upon time, a group of non-speciesist humans got together to change or reinterpret their religion or ideology so that humans had a new justification for exploiting nonhuman animals for things like food, clothing, and labor. Instead, though it is likely humans have some vegetarian ancestors, long before we had capacity for serious moral reflection our relatives found that they could survive and thrive by exploiting other animals. Clough concludes, "And because they could, they did." It was simply a matter of raw power that needed no ideological justification or motivation.

Ever since that time, Clough says, almost all human beings have been born into cultures that exploit animals to survive and thrive. When our ancestors eventually reached a stage of development in which we could reflect morally on how we treated animals, philosophers and other thinkers developed ideas and arguments meant to explain the difference between humans and animals in order to justify this behavior. But human exploitation of animals is tens of thousands of years older than any philosophical or religious rationale for such exploitation. Human beings used other animals for their own purposes because they had the power to do so—just as human groups with power have subjugated African Americans, women, and prenatal human beings.

Clough acknowledges that certain Christian thinkers have been among those who developed and promoted speciesist ideas and practices. But since human beings are fallen, selfish, and violent creatures, it should come as no surprise that imperfect and sinful members of the Christian churches, in common with other traditions of thought (many of them secular), have often preferred to read their texts and doctrines in ways that justify speciesist exploitation of animals. But our exploitation of animals was not, and is not, motivated by ideas or texts. As our history shows, it needs no ideological motivation. Powerful humans wanted to survive and thrive, and used vulnerable animals (and other humans) toward this end because they could. End of story.

Clough is quick to point out that it is still important to challenge religious and philosophical justifications of this exploitation. (Indeed, that is much of what is going on in the first half of this book.) But challenging such rationales is only the first step in changing the way we live our lives. Because speciesism needs no moral justification for most people, it is also necessary to restrict the choice and power of those who would benefit from treating animals unjustly.

Christianity as the Bad Guy, Part II: Lynn White, Jr.

OK, so history tells us that Christian thought is not the basis for speciesism or exploitation of animals in the Western world. But perhaps the actual charge should be something more specific. Perhaps we should say instead that Christianity is responsible for *the particular way* in which we exploit animals in our culture. This was the argument of Lynn White, Jr., a professor of medieval history who taught at Princeton, Stanford, and UCLA over the course of his career. In a famous article called "The Historical Roots of Our Ecological Crisis," White begins with his concern that our current technological practices are threatening human life and the ecological balance in very dangerous ways. Like Singer, his response is to go back to foundational ideas and try to rethink them in the hopes of avoiding an ecological crisis.

If we were to pick a time in history during which we first had massive-scale technology that significantly affected the earth's ecology, most would pick the revolution in science and technology in sixteenth- and seventeenth-century Europe. But White claims that we can find examples hundreds of years before this: for instance, when humans first used water and wind to power machines on a large scale. In fact, White reminds us, technology had developed during the Middle Ages such that very small and (previously) weak countries in Europe were in a position to dominate and colonize much of the non-Western world by the end of the 1400s.

White argues that our understanding of technology (and its relationship to nature) got its start and justification not from the secular Enlightenment and Industrial Revolution, but from the religious thought of the Middle Ages. The Christian culture, in White's view, replaced a pagan culture that was far less exploitive of nature. Christian theology replaced a pagan understanding of a world in which all things had a spiritual reality—a reality human beings were forced to acknowledge and consider before they mined a mountain, damned a brook, or even cut down a tree. Christianity, by contrast, rejected the spiritual reality of all creation and claimed that human beings alone are made in the image of God and have souls. According to White, Christian theology even insists that God commands humanity to exploit and subdue the natural world. And it is this view that has been passed on to even secular Westerners today.

But let's bring this conversation back to animals. We learned from Clough's response to Singer that Christian thought is not responsible for speciesism from the beginning. But given White's argument, couldn't one argue that Christianity is responsible for the massive technological and speciesist exploitation of animals that we have today? After all, if we had kept the pagan view that all animals have a spiritual nature worth respecting, and rejected the view that God wills us to exploit the earth's resources, perhaps large-scale factory farms and animal laboratories would be less acceptable.

Responding to White

Like Singer, White is not a theologian and he also makes serious mistakes in his analysis of history and Christian theology. As we will see in future chapters, he misinterprets much of the Bible—which has almost nothing to say about technology. But for now, let's look carefully at White's key claim: He says that Christianity's replacing of paganism marked a fundamental shift when it comes to humans exploiting the natural world around them. How does this claim stand up to history? Unfortunately for White, and much like Singer's claim that Christianity is responsible for speciesism, the answer is not very well.

University of Notre Dame professor Joseph Blenkinsopp has taken great care in addressing White's claims from a historical point of view, and he makes a point similar to Clough's. Exploitation of nature, even on a massive scale, was not motivated by anything said in the Bible or, indeed, any religious tradition. Our ecological world was being devastated and living species were being destroyed long before Christianity came around. Blenkinsopp gives examples of such exploitation that were wholly unrelated to religious practices or ideas—like the systematic destruction of the cedar forests in Lebanon and the hunting of the Syrian elephant to extinction (circa 2000 B.C. and 700 B.C., respectively). If the

Assyrians had the technology of the Industrial Revolution, notes Blenkinsopp, they would have been even more destructive. In rare cases we find that religious practices are connected to the exploitation of nature, but it is mostly an accidental side effect rather than the consequence of the religious ideology itself. (He gives the example of the deforesting of India resulting from the cremation required by Hinduism and Buddhism.) Since the Bible, again, has little to say about technology, we are actually better off looking elsewhere for the historical roots of our ecological crisis.

We should never forget history's lesson that exploitation of nature—and of animals—needs no ideological justification. This is true whether we are discussing hunting the Syrian elephant in 700 B.C. or factory farming pigs in A.D. 2014. Humans are sinful, fallen, and selfish creatures who will use their power to exploit those who are weaker, regardless of the age in which we live. If we are going to talk about a new kind of exploitation going on in our own time, however, perhaps we should point to the development of individualism during the Enlightenment and the consumerism brought on by the Industrial Revolution as the turning points. These events paved the way for humanity to ignore or deny the fact that we live under a creator and must respect that Creator's creation. In this view, our place in the universe is truly dominant, and limited only by the mechanisms of the market, not the law of a Creator God.

On this point Christianity has an unlikely ally. In his book *How Are We to Live? Ethics in an Age of Self-Interest*, Peter Singer rightly points out that the Christian tradition is actually very suspicious of moneymaking as an enterprise. St. Gregory the Great claimed that it stained one's soul, while St. Leo the Great warned that it was difficult to avoid sin when buying and selling as a profession. Exploitive lending of money at interest, called usury (the predatory loans which caused our recent financial crisis is a classic example of this), was considered intrinsically evil and punishable by excommunication from the Church. This is in stark contrast to secular thinkers of the Enlightenment—such as Adam Smith and Benjamin Franklin—who argued that it could be a proper goal of life to use the market to become wealthy.

A consumerist push for profit and moneymaking is what drives the massive and speciesist exploitation of animals in today's factory farms. Sellers of meat (in part, once again, because consumers are so disconnected from their food sources that their primary concern is buying it at the right price) participate in a market that forces them to do everything they can to bring costs down. Unfortunately for many animals, this means that they will be exploited in torturous conditions in order to produce the most meat at the lowest cost to the seller. Ideology—and especially Christian theology—is absent from the equation. It is rather about raw power. Factory farmers can exploit animals in this way, and so they do.

Christianity, though an imperfect tradition with respect to animals, is certainly not responsible for our speciesist practices on either a small scale or a large scale. Though this an important point to get straight here at the beginning of this book, there are still other important questions to ask. It is one thing, after all, to say that Christianity is not responsible for the problem, but it is quite another to say (as I do throughout this book) that it is *part of the solution*. Despite the conclusion of this chapter, might Christianity nevertheless be so infected with speciesism that it cannot be a tool of liberation for animals? We might be tempted to answer yes, especially if we think that the Christian tradition claims that human beings are at the center or pinnacle of God's creation, with all other creatures below them. It is to this question we turn in the next chapter.

QUESTIONS FOR DISCUSSION

1. Why do you think many traditional Christians are skeptical of those who want more ethical concern for animals?
2. When do you think humans started exploiting animals? Do you think it was taken up a notch at any point in history? The Middle Ages? The Industrial Revolution? Some other time?
3. Is it fair to say that human beings are sinful creatures who will often, for their own advantage, exploit those over whom they have power?
4. Is it fair to say that market forces driving down the cost of meat force meat sellers to treat animals poorly in order to compete?

SUGGESTIONS FOR FURTHER READING

Animal Liberation: A New Ethics for Our Treatment of Animals by Peter Singer

"The Historical Roots of Our Ecological Crisis" by Lynn White, Jr., in *Ecology and Religion in History*

On Animals: Systematic Theology by David L. Clough

Peter Singer and Christian Ethics: Beyond Polarization by Charles C. Camosy (especially chapter three, "Animals")

"Toward an Ethic of Limitation" by Joseph Blenkinsopp, in *The Challenge of Global Stewardship*, edited by Maura Ryan and Todd Whitmore

The Wealth of Nations by Adam Smith

CHRISTIANITY AND THE NONHUMAN: FROM ANGELS TO ALIENS

IN THE PREVIOUS CHAPTER, WE saw how internationally important and influential thinkers like Peter Singer and Lynn White, Jr., operate with a big assumption—an assumption, sadly, that is shared by most Christians. Large majorities of secularists and believers think the Bible tells us that the human being is the most important and highest being in creation. The rest of creation is meant, in some capacity, to serve human wants and needs. After all, didn't God give human beings dominion over the earth and command us to subdue it?

In the last chapter we saw that Christianity is not the originator of speciesist ideas like this. But I want this book to show not only that Christian thought is not the problem, but also that it is part of the solution. This seems like a tough sell, however, given that the Bible appears to have set up a situation in which humans are to dominate and use animals and the rest of creation. But in this pivotal chapter I hope to convince you of two points that are absolutely essential for the main argument of this book. First, the relationship between humans and the rest of creation is far more complicated than this: *Dominion* in a Christian theological context doesn't mean what many think it means. Second, the best Christian sources strongly resist the view that creation exists merely for human beings or that human beings stand at the highest point of creation.

In order to make my case, I will begin by exploring in more detail what Christianity has to say about the point of creation and the role human beings are understood to play. I will then turn to the neglected topic of angels: a group of nonhuman beings that the Christian tradition understands as higher than humans in many different ways. Finally, I will highlight other nonhuman creatures recognized by the Christian tradition who, like angels, are also rational, self-aware, and capable of knowledge and love. These will include everything from the giants mentioned in the book of Genesis to the aliens mentioned in the theological schools of the Middle Ages, and even by the Vatican today.

What Is Creation For?

The answer given by many Christians is that creation is for human beings. It is like the background scenery for a play in which the fall, salvation, and redemption of human beings is being acted out. Some might say that this scenery is absolutely necessary: God seems to have used evolution, for instance, to produce human beings, the stars of the drama. But what really matters is the actors in the play, not the scenery. David Clough, mentioned in the last chapter as the British Christian ethicist who showed that Christianity is not responsible for speciesism in the West, calls this the "it's all about us" position. The problem for such a position is that our best Christian sources, when we look at them carefully, tell a very different story.

As Clough notes in his new book *On Animals: Systematic*

Theology, the Bible really doesn't tell us much about the reason God created the universe. It mainly focuses on celebrating the fact that God in fact did this wondrous thing. When God speaks to Job in the whirlwind, for instance, God makes no attempt to explain the rationale for creation. Instead, he insists that Job should react in wonder and awe to its majesty and diversity. Christians are told in the beginning of John's Gospel (among other places) that all things were made through the Word of God, Jesus Christ, but we are not told the purpose of creation.

That the Bible is virtually silent on this question has not stopped others from speculating. The Jewish philosopher Philo of Alexandria, who lived during the time of Jesus, was one of the most influential people in the "it's all about us" camp—and his thought would go on to justify many others (including Christians) in this camp throughout the centuries. The problem is that Philo gets much of his view of creation from the views of Plato, a pagan Greek philosopher who claimed that the world was created for human persons, and that all nonpersons (everything from human females to birds to fish) were deficient in some way. Indeed, Philo is troubled by the fact that the Bible doesn't always seem to match up well with Plato's philosophy and spends much of his writing trying to explain this away. Unfortunately for a Bible-focused understanding of creation, many Christian thinkers (Gregory of Nyssa, John Chrysostom, Bonaventure, Martin Luther, John Calvin, and more) simply borrowed the view of Philo until it became a virtually unquestioned part of the Christian tradition.

There are other Christian thinkers in the "it's all about us" camp, but Clough rightly notes that these were either justified by other kinds of pagan thought (appeals were often made to the

Stoics and Gnostics), or no argument was given at all. But it is high time that Christians take a more careful look at our best sources on this question and have these be our foundation. The very first sentences of the Bible tell us that all of creation—from light to plants to animals—is created "good." Period. No reference to human beings at all. When human beings are referenced later on, we learn that they are made in the image of God and have a particular role in creation, but Genesis is clear that the world is not created for human beings. Indeed, all creatures have goodness independent of human beings.

Other Christian thinkers argue that God made creation, not for humanity, but for God's own glory. Clough cites huge theological names like Thomas Aquinas and Karl Barth as taking this position, but then highlights some problems with it. First, and most obviously, God has no need to receive glory from us, from frogs, or from anything else in creation. Second, this position paints a picture of a God that is self-obsessed and ungracious: very different from the self-giving (even unto death) God revealed in the person of Jesus Christ. God's creative act, if it is truly though Jesus Christ, is a self-giving act of love and fellowship. While human beings have an important and perhaps unique place in God's fellowship with creation, if we take the Bible seriously then we must admit that God's loving act of creation produces creatures with goodness that cannot be reduced to the good of human beings.

Catholic Teaching on Creation
Some Catholic readers might find all of this interesting, but still wonder what the Church has to say about these matters. Well, it turns out that Catholic teaching not only rejects the "it's all

about us" position, but affirms much of what Clough argues. The *Compendium of the Social Doctrine of the Church* insists that the earth has a "prior God-given purpose" which human beings "must not betray." This is a moral duty, says the Church, which extends to "every economic activity making use of natural resources." According to Pope Benedict XVI in his authoritative encyclical *Caritas in Veritate*, this means we must adopt "new life-styles" which resist consumerism as the primary way we relate to the earth. The pope, citing Genesis 9:12, reminds us that that there is a covenant between human beings and creation which must govern our behavior. Violation of this covenant is now seen as one of seven new "deadly sins" described by the Vatican in 2008.

The idea that humans are bound by a covenant with creation such that we must change our consumerist lifestyles would be enough all by itself to provide a challenge to the "it's all about us" view. But wait, there's more. Unlike the ecological concern of thinkers like Peter Singer—who find it difficult to talk about the objective moral value of anything that cannot suffer—the *Catechism of the Catholic Church* (333–337) takes Genesis 1 seriously and says that "the whole of creation" has an inner nature and value. God, the *Catechism* says, has created all things as "interdependent" and concludes, "no creature is self-sufficient." Remarkably, we are also told that the "Word of God and his Breath are at the origin of the being and life of every creature (703)." The earth and its nonhuman creatures are not *more* important than are human creatures, but this is perfectly consistent with the *Compendium*'s teaching (which cites Romans 8:19–23) that "the whole of creation" participates in the redemption of Jesus Christ.

The "it's all about us" view has far more to do with our natural human tendency toward self-obsession, and with pagan philosophy, than with fundamentally Christian ideas. But to drive this point home let's take a closer look how Christians over the centuries and up until the present day have understood nonhuman beings. And let's start with a group of beings that are nearly forgotten in our (intellectual) culture: angels.

Angels

Most contemporary intellectuals don't think about angels at all—except, perhaps, when it is time to decorate the top of the Christmas tree. During both my doctoral studies in theology and during my time in the academic world as a professor I've encountered only two people who put any time at all into thinking and writing about angels. Unsurprisingly, few of us know much about them. How many Catholics, for instance, are even aware that each year we celebrate the Feast of the Archangels Michael, Gabriel, and Raphael? The reality of angels isn't even emphasized on their own feast day, much less throughout the Church year.

When asked whether they believe in angels, however, a solid majority of Americans (some estimates are as high as 75 percent) claim that they do. There are even credible stories run by major news outlets that explore whether angels have acted in certain situations. In late 2008, for instance, NBC News covered the following story:

> A 14-year-old girl with a history of serious health issues lay dying of pneumonia in a hospital room. But as her mother waited for the girl to take her last breath, an image of bright light appeared on a security monitor. Within an hour, the

dying girl began a recovery that doctors are at a loss to explain.

But Colleen Banton, the girl's mother, has an explanation. "This was an image of an angel," she told NBC News in a story reported Tuesday on TODAY. She credited the apparition with saving the life of her daughter Chelsea.

Chelsea and her mother were told by physicians that there was no hope. But NBC reported that non-family members—"including nurses who were on duty"—said the three vertical shafts present in the hospital were indisputably an angel. Indeed, after the event Chelsea got better in ways that defy medical explanation.

If you live in the developed world, and especially if you have a college education, you are likely skeptical about the claims of the mother and the nurse staff. At a different time in history, however—before secularism was able to convince Western culture that science had the answer to every question worth asking—it would have been obvious that an angel healed this girl. And this is still true for countercultural others (especially traditional Muslims and those living outside the developed West) who make room for the possibility of spiritual, nonhuman beings operating in our world. Indeed, the archangel Raphael (an important part of the traditions of Judaism, Christianity, and Islam) is known both in the Bible and the Quran precisely for his healing power, and is sometimes called "the medicine of God." He remains the patron saint of the sick.

In the Christian tradition, angels are present not only at miraculous times, they are all around us impacting many aspects of our lives. St. Bonaventure, a Franciscan friar from the Middle Ages, took it for granted that angels are "circling around us like flies."

Oxford University's David Albert Jones reminds us in his book *Angels: A Very Short Introduction* that Jesus suggests each of us has a guardian angel. Recall Jesus saying, "Take care that you do not despise one of these little ones; for, I tell you, in heaven their angels continually see the face of my Father in heaven" (Matthew 18:10). Jones also helpfully recounts how angels, and perhaps our guardian angels, are thought to be present from the beginning of our lives. This tradition arises out the biblical accounts of angels announcing the births of Isaac (Genesis 18:10; Quran 51:28), Ishmael (Genesis 16:11), Samson (Judges 13:3), John the Baptist (Luke 1:18; Quran 3.39), and Jesus (Luke 1:26-27; Quran 3:45). A sobering thought—but perhaps a comforting one as well—is that angels (and, again, perhaps our guardian angels) are thought to be present at our deaths. This tradition has its roots with Jesus's saying that Lazarus was carried by an angel to the bosom of Abraham (Luke 16:22). Angels, it should be clear by now, are anything but rare characters in Scripture. Marco Bussagli's book *Angels* has helpful chapters on each book in which angels appear. It is quite the list:

Genesis

Exodus

Numbers

Joshua

Judges

1 Samuel

1 Kings

2 Kings

Tobit

Judith

2 Maccabees

Job

Psalms

Proverbs

Wisdom

Isaiah

Ezekiel

Daniel

Matthew

Mark

Luke

John

Acts

Ephesians

Colossians

1 Peter

2 Peter

Revelation

How Are Angels Different from Humans?

We've said a number of things about angels so far, but it still might
not be clear what angels are. And, to tell the truth, though the
Christian tradition is quite clear about the fact that angels exist,
it is less clear about the nature of angels. We can say a few things
about them with some confidence, however. Angels are "rational
beings" which, according to Christian tradition, means that they
have the capacity to know and to love. Angels also have a will
and can make moral or immoral choices: indeed, according to
tradition, some of those choices got Lucifer and others kicked out
of heaven. Angels have different jobs and seem to have different

personalities to fit those jobs. Michael, for instance, is defender of God and has the personality of a warrior—but Raphael, as a healer, has a different role and personality. Angels share traits such as personality, will, morality, knowing, and loving in common with human beings. We shouldn't be surprised about this, however, especially when Jesus himself says that after the resurrection human beings become "like angels in heaven" (Mark 12:25).

Though they are similar to us in several ways, angels are different from human beings. Importantly for the topic of this chapter, angels stand above human beings in the hierarchy of creation. Psalm 8, for example, declares that God has made human beings lower than the angels. What makes angels higher than humans? The tradition isn't clear on this point. The great theologian of the Middle Ages, Thomas Aquinas, thought that the main difference was that angels had direct knowledge from God, whereas human beings come to know one thing via something else. For example, we come to know God through Scripture or the witness of the saints, but angels come to know God (and other things) directly without the need for an intermediate step. Many also think of angels as purely spiritual creatures, while humans have bodies. But in some places it seems as though angels have bodies as well, such as when Jacob wrestles with the angel (Genesis 32:24–30) or when Abraham eats with three angels (Genesis 18:1–5).

So, according to the Christian tradition, angels and humans— though different—are not different kinds of things. Both angels and humans, at bottom, are things that are capable of knowing and loving God. Angels do this more excellently than humans, but both do it. Indeed, the Christian tradition has described both angels and humans as "substances of a rational nature." That is, both are persons. Angels, according to Christianity, are *nonhuman* persons. The concept of a "nonhuman person" may sound strange to our speciesist ears, but upon reflection it is rather common in our books and movies. After all, who could doubt that Superman and Bilbo Baggins are classic and obvious examples of nonhuman persons? The nonhuman person is also common in many places of the Christian tradition, not just with respect to angels.

Neither Angel nor Human?

Throughout the Christian tradition, other creatures with a rational nature are discussed who do not appear to be either humans or angels. At the beginning of Genesis 6, for instance, we are told that beings called the "sons of God" came down to earth and managed to have sex with the "daughters of men"—and even produced children. The passage says that these children were "giants" or "the Nephilim." Though not human, they were certainly persons, and even described as renowned warriors of old. Furthermore, Christian historian Franklin Harkins points out that many of the best thinkers in the Christian tradition were convinced that a male or female demon (*incubus* or *succubus*) could also have sex with human beings. Harkins notes that Albert the Great (the teacher of Thomas Aquinas) claimed that many in his social circle heard stories about this taking place. Albert himself claimed to know someone who cannot even sleep through a single night without a "demonic *succubus* coming to him."

Consider also that many Christian thinkers believed that there were creatures called *homines* in unknown parts of the earth, who were biologically different from humans. There was a particular focus on creatures, otherwise human, who had the heads of dogs. These *cynocephali* certainly had a rational nature, and even formed communities with towns, agriculture, and the rule of law. These creatures are found pictured in many pieces of Christian art—some of which even show Christ preaching to these dog-headed creatures. According to some legends, St. Christopher himself was thought to be a cynocephalus (we can find icons of him with the head of a dog) before he was rewarded with full human form for aiding the Christ-child.

What about Aliens?
David Albert Jones makes an interesting connection between angels and aliens. He says that our secular doctrines cause many of us to reject belief in angels, but the concept of aliens has stepped up to take its place. In the 1970s, for instance, the alien enthusiast Eric Von Daniken caused a controversy by claiming that Abraham and Jacob did not meet angels, but aliens. For Jones, this is but one of dozens of examples of materialist tradition trying to fill the human need for spiritualty. Many of us probably know someone who is just plain fanatical about their belief in aliens, even to the point where it seems like something close to religious belief. If Jones is correct, then aliens are angels for modern people who cannot imagine anything beyond the physical.

Few are aware of it, but consideration of aliens (separate from angels) has a significant history within the Christian tradition. Tom O'Meara, emeritus professor of theology at the University of Notre Dame, wrote *Vast Universe: Extraterrestials and Christian Revelation*, which contains an interesting summary of this history. The pre-Christian Greeks and Romans speculated on the possibility of other worlds, but few thought about nonhuman persons living on them. O'Meara notes that, though the Christian tradition offers mixed views on whether there are or could be persons on other planets, some were actually encouraged to believe in the possibility of aliens on the basis of their Christian convictions.

As early as the third century, the great theologian Origen saw the saving action of Jesus as a kind of cosmic drama which avoided a self-centered focus on humans and earth, and included multiple worlds and intelligent beings. The Franciscian school of the Middle Ages also took up the question of multiple worlds, but even more directly and specifically than did Origen. Bonaventure, for instance, explicitly claimed that God may have created such worlds. The Franciscian friar Guillaume de Vaurouillon, a professor of theology at the University of Paris, took up these questions more seriously than anyone else in the Middle Ages. He apparently thought it was likely that multiple worlds existed, but believed they were so far away that only angels or direct revelation from God could reveal them to us. He also explicitly claimed Jesus Christ's salvation could reach the inhabitants of such worlds.

By the beginning of the Renaissance, this was an open topic for discussion. We have Roman Catholic cardinals like Nicholas of Cusa, for instance, being very explicit in saying, "We surmise that none of the other regions of the stars is empty of inhabitants." In addition, advances in astronomy led the Baroque Scholastics to speculate further on the possibility of rational biological life in worlds other than ours. The great philosopher and theologian Francisco Suarez, for instance, claimed that an incarnation of God could take place more than once and that the object of Christian love should be "every rational creature" or every creature that is capable of grasping its own satisfaction.

Modern Catholic Thought on Aliens

Late in the twentieth century, theologians like Teilhard de Chardin, Yves Congar, and Karl Rahner addressed the implication of aliens on other worlds in some detail—and even thinking about their salvation much like the Church came to think about the salvation of non-Christians on Earth. Today, even Rome is in on the conversation. The Vatican Observatory and the Pontifical Academy of Sciences recently hosted its second conference on astrobiology (the study of life beyond earth) in five years. The director of the observatory, Fr. Jose Funes, S.J., said, "the questions of life's origins and of whether life exists elsewhere in the universe are very interesting and deserve serious consideration." One of the pope's personal astronomers, Fr. Guy Consolmagno, said he would be "delighted" if intelligent life was found among the stars and would even baptize an alien "if he asked."

We began this chapter by asking whether Christianity could actually be helpful in getting beyond our culture's self-obsessed, speciesist focus on the human. And we have seen not only that each creature is created "good" independent of human interests, but that human beings are not even the center or highest part of creation. Indeed, the Christian tradition understands human beings to be some of *the lowest* kinds of persons God created—ranking below a great variety of angelic creatures with a rational nature. We also discovered that, even beyond angels, the tradition makes room for other nonhuman persons: demons, giants, cynocephali, and even aliens.

So what does this have to do with animals? At a minimum, it is overwhelming evidence that Christians should drop the speciesist view that nonhuman creatures are mere "things" for us to do with as we please. Christianity requires that we reject the idea that animals exist primarily as resources for us—without any sense of the goodness God has given them independent of human beings. But there is another important insight to gather from this chapter, and it pushes us to challenge the human vs. animal distinction. When we claim someone is "acting like an animal" most often we are criticizing him or her. Animals are put into the "other" category, associated with the negative. But in light of what we find in this chapter, this cannot be a Christian understanding. Human beings are also created as animals. Rational animals, yes, but animals nonetheless. Given that we now know that the Christian tradition makes room for nonhuman persons, is it possible that some animals are nonhuman persons? It would be unjust speciesism to rule out other animals without even investigating the question. We will do this investigation in chapter eight, but for now it is enough to simply say that the question is legitimate and should be taken seriously by Christians.

From now on, instead of using the term *animal*, I will more often use the term *nonhuman animal*. This will remind us not only that we humans are animals, but also that we should not set up the terms *animal* and *human* in binary opposition to each other, as if, somehow, the more human the better, and the more animal the worse. As the *Catechism of the Catholic Church* says, both human and nonhuman animals are created with the breath of life.

Adding to the moral status and value of nonhuman animals need not take away the value of human beings—unless you (wrongly) set up the terms in opposition to each other. As we saw in chapter one, being successful in acquiring justice for certain vulnerable populations did not hurt the moral status of other populations. Justice is not a zero-sum game. Even if we found that there are some nonhuman persons on our planet and decided to treat them with justice, this would not threaten the standing of human persons—at least no more than recognizing the personhood of African Americans and women threatens the moral status of white men, and no more than recognizing the value of prenatal children threatens the moral status of those who are already born.

Questions for Discussion

1. In your experience, does Christianity teach that creation and animals were made to serve the interests of human beings? After seeing the evidence presented in this chapter, do you still believe that? Why or why not?

2. If all creation is "good," without reference to human beings, what does this mean for ecological or environmental concern?

3. Do you think about angels and how they impact your life? Why or why not? Why do you think so little is made of angels today?

4. What is meant when we say that someone is "acting like an animal"? Is this a helpful way of thinking about the relationship between human and nonhuman animals?

5. Do you think there could be nonhuman persons? Are Superman and Bilbo Baggins examples of this? Is it possible that some nonhuman animals are persons?

Suggestions for Further Reading

Angels by Marco Bussagli
Angels: A Very Short Introduction by David Albert Jones

On Animals: Systematic Theology by David L. Clough

Caritas in Veritate by Pope Benedict XVI

Compendium of the Social Doctrine of the Church by the Pontifical Council for Justice and Peace

"The Embodiment of Angels: A Debate in Mid-Thirteenth Century Theology" by Franklin Harkins, in *Recherche de et Theologie Philosophie Medievales*

"The Historical Roots of Our Ecological Crisis" by Lynn White, Jr., in *Ecology and Religion in History*

"Intellectual Strangers No More? Peter Singer and Roman Catholicism on Ecological Concern" by Charles Camosy, in *Claritas: The Journal of Dialogue and Culture*

Practical Ethics by Peter Singer

Ten Commandments for the Environment: Pope Benedict Speaks Out for Creation and Justice by Woodene Koenig-Bricker

Vast Universe: Extraterrestrials and Christian Revelation by Thomas F. O'Meara

CHAPTER FOUR

ANIMALS AND THE BIBLE

WE ARE NOW PREPARED TO dive more deeply into discussion of nonhuman animals and the Christian tradition. We have learned, among other things, that the tradition is not responsible for our culture's speciesism and that it does not think of all of creation as merely existing for the sake of human beings. But the next three chapters will show that Christianity has much more to say about nonhuman animals than this. Chapter six will highlight current teachings and ideas about nonhuman animals, chapter five will explore the tradition of the saints and other people close to God, and this chapter will explore what Scripture has to say. Consideration of the Bible will be of interest not only to Evangelical Christians, but also to us Catholic Christians who, especially after the Second Vatican Council, moved to ground our theology in Scripture.

Of course, we have already discussed some of what Scripture has to say about nonhuman animals—at least indirectly. We saw in Genesis that God creates nonhuman animals "good" in their own right and without any reference to human beings, for instance. But there are still many more questions to explore. For example, we briefly noted that God gives humans dominion over all creation, but what does this dominion mean if nonhuman animals are created good, independent of human beings? Also, Jesus ate fish and may have eaten meat. Paul appears to reject the intrinsic value of nonhuman animals. Peter has a vision in which he was commanded by God to eat meat. And didn't God demand killing nonhuman animals for sacrifice? We will attempt to answer these and other challenges in the second part of this chapter, but first let us look at the support the Bible gives for the moral status of nonhuman animals. Brace yourselves: Some of what we are about to consider may surprise you.

Biblical Support for the Moral Status of Animals

Let's just say this right up front: The Bible, from its beginnings, is far more concerned with nonhuman animals (and their relationship with humans) than our secular culture is today. In the very first sentences of the Bible, for instance, we get lots of insight into a theological approach to nonhuman animals. Let's take close look at the sixth day of creation and examine details that are often passed over too quickly:

> And God said, "Let the earth bring forth living creatures of every kind: cattle and creeping things and wild animals of the earth of every kind." And it was so. God made the wild animals of the earth of every kind, and the cattle of every kind, and everything that creeps upon the ground of every kind. And God saw that it was good.
>
> Then God said, "'Let us make humankind in our image, according to our likeness; and let them have dominion over the fish of the sea, and over the birds of the air, and over the cattle, and over all the wild animals of the earth, and over every creeping thing that creeps upon the earth."

So God created humankind in his image,

in the image of God he created them;

male and female he created them.

God blessed them, and God said to them, "Be fruitful and multiply, and fill the earth and subdue it; and have dominion over the fish of the sea and over the birds of the air and over every living thing that moves upon the earth." God said, "See, I have given you every plant yielding seed that is upon the face of all the earth, and every tree with seed in its fruit; you shall have them for food. And to every beast of the earth, and to every bird of the air, and to everything that creeps on the earth, everything that has the breath of life, I have given every green plant for food." And it was so. God saw everything that he had made, and indeed, it was very good. And there was evening and there was morning, the sixth day. (Genesis 1:24–31)

First, let us again drive home a point that cannot be made often enough: Nonhuman animals are pronounced "good" by God without reference to human beings and even before human beings are created. Second, let's think about the relationship implied between humans and nonhuman animals here. Are nonhuman animals created to be our food? Not at all. In fact, God explicitly gives us fruit and vegetables to eat. (It is only much later, after sin has entered the world, that God gives limited permission to eat meat and wear animal skin.) Genesis 2 gives us further evidence by explaining the relationship God intends for human and nonhuman animals to have. One again, the claims that animals are brought to Adam because he is hungry or because he needs help with manual labor are missing. Instead, we are told that they animals are brought to him because "it is not good that man should be alone." Animals, at least according to God's will, are intended to be Adam's companions.

Let's also note the fact that human and nonhuman animals are created on the same day, implying a kind of special relationship or kinship. Earlier we saw that *Catechism* understands both human and nonhuman animals to have the "breath of life"; this interpretation has strong support from the third chapter of Ecclesiastes:

> I said in my heart with regard to human beings that God is testing them to show that they are but animals. For the fate of human beings and the fate of animals is the same; as one dies, so dies the other. They all have the same breath, and humans have no advantage over the animals; for all is vanity. (Ecclesiastes 3:18–20)

In a moment we will lay out some challenges to the view that there is a biblical mandate to consider the moral status of nonhuman animals. Whatever one thinks of these challenges, the Bible is clear that our current violent and predatory relationship with other animals is problematic, certainly not the moral ideal and, a temporary situation. The prophets Isaiah, Ezekiel, and Hosea all predict a return to the nonviolence of Eden. Here is the way this peaceful kingdom is envisioned in the eleventh chapter of Isaiah. In my opinion, it is among the most moving and hopeful parts of the Bible:

> The wolf shall live with the lamb,
>   the leopard shall lie down with the kid,
>   the calf and the lion and the fatling together,
>   and a little child shall lead them.

The cow and the bear shall graze,
    their young shall lie down together;
    and the lion shall eat straw like the ox.

The nursing child shall play over the hole of the asp,
    and the weaned child shall put its hand on the adder's den.

They will not hurt or destroy
    on all my holy mountain;
for the earth will be full of the knowledge of the LORD
    as the waters cover the sea. (Isaiah 11:6–9)

God's will from the beginning, and even now looking forward to the end of times, is peace and nonviolence for all creation. Many of us say the Lord's Prayer on a regular basis; this, of course, is the prayer which calls for God's will to be done on earth as it is in heaven. God's will for nonhuman animals is clear: They are to be our companions, not our food. We are to live together in a peaceful kingdom ruled by the peace-loving God revealed to us through Jesus Christ. Theologians like Stanley Hauerwas and John Berkman ask us to confront the following challenge: Can Christians be witnesses to the world that creation is not meant to be at war with itself? Can we live our lives according to the new peaceful order of Jesus, the Prince of Peace, instead of the old order of violence?

Doesn't God Permit Meat-Eating and Animal Sacrifice?

For those who are familiar with Scripture, there are a number of other places that seem to push in a different direction. What do we do, for instance, with Genesis 9 where human beings are told that the "fear and dread of you shall rest on every animal of the earth, and on every bird of the air, on everything that creeps on the ground, and on all the fish of the sea; into your hand they are delivered. Every moving thing that lives shall be food for you"? Whatever God may have intended originally, what we have here is something very different. And how tragically true this prediction turned out to be: The fear and dread present in the suffering of the tens of billions of nonhuman animals tortured and killed every year in factory farms exists on a scale the ancient world couldn't possibly imagine. This seems like a very different problem to overcome for those who, like me, believe Scripture provides support for seeing nonhuman animals as part of the peaceful Kingdom of God.

One important response to this passage comes from the Anglican priest Andrew Linzey, who has been a voice crying in the Christian wilderness for decades on these issues. Linzey reminds us that the permission to eat nonhuman animals is granted only after God has brought a flood to destroy the world. Genesis 6 contains a stinging indictment of humanity:

> Now the earth was corrupt in God's sight, and the earth was filled with violence. And God saw that the earth was corrupt; for all flesh had corrupted its ways upon the earth. And God said to Noah, "I have determined to make an end of all flesh, for the earth is filled with violence because of them...." (Genesis 6:11–13)

God was particularly angered by the violence that had permeated the earth. Linzey says that the "ambiguous permission" to eat animals needs to be seen in the context of accommodation to human sinfulness and, in particular, human violence. But that accommodation is certainly not unlimited and certainly not consistent with how many Christians treat nonhuman animals today. Despite this permission, God puts limits on when and how we can kill nonhuman animals for food—for instance, there is the prohibition against eating an animal still containing its "life blood." This is a reminder that we may kill only with the understanding that the life we take does not belong to us, but belongs to God. Indeed, Linzey says that there is no *right* to kill and eat nonhuman animals, for God allows it only under the conditions of necessity. Interestingly, this view mirrors the teaching of the *Catechism*, which (as we will see in chapter six) claims that we may only cause nonhuman animals to suffer and die in situations of great need.

But what about ritual sacrifice? If there is one thing we know from the Hebrew Bible, it is that nonhuman animals were sacrificed to God. At times it even looks like God even provides for this to happen. Many readers will be familiar with Genesis 22 where God stops Abraham from sacrificing his son Isaac and provides a ram to kill and sacrifice instead. How is this example, and many dozens of others involving ritual sacrifice of nonhuman animals, consistent with the moral status of such animals as part of the peaceful Kingdom of God?

The most likely explanation is that this sacrifice was a holdover from the influence of the practices of Israel's pagan neighbors, and not the will of the peaceful God revealed in Jesus Christ. Later, the Hebrew prophets insist that God does not desire the sacrifice of nonhuman animals. Consider the following three typical condemnations:

"What to me is the multitude of your sacrifices?
    says the LORD;
I have had enough of burnt offerings of rams
    and the fat of fed beasts;
I do not delight in the blood of bulls,
    or of lambs, or of goats. (Isaiah 1:11)

For I desire steadfast love and not sacrifice,
    the knowledge of God rather than burnt offerings. (Hosea
    6:6)

Even thought you offer me your burnt offerings and grain
offerings,
    I will not accept them;
and the offerings of well-being of your fatted animals
    I will not look upon.
Take away from me the noise of your songs;
    I will not listen to the melody of your harps.
But let justice roll down like waters,
    and righteousness like an ever-flowing stream. (Amos
    5:22–24)

The earliest Christians were strongly connected to Judaism and had to decide how much of the Jewish Law they were going to uphold. There was a famous disagreement between Peter and Paul on precisely this question. The Church's important compromise, which according to Acts 15 seems to have been brokered by James (the "brother of the Lord" who was in charge of the Church at Jerusalem), was that Christians should keep the following four practices:

1. Abstain from meat sacrificed to idols
2. Abstain from sexual immorality
3. Abstain from meat from strangled animals
4. Abstain from meat with the animal's life blood still inside
   it

The ritual sacrifice of nonhuman animals is nowhere to be seen, and three of the four prohibitions that remain involve refraining from killing and eating nonhuman animals. Prohibitions 3 and 4 are of particular interest for us given that they show explicit respect for the moral status of nonhuman animals. Jewish law was actually quite strict about how nonhuman animals were to be killed, right down to regulations about using a blade sharp enough that death would be instantaneous. Not surprisingly, in prohibition 3 we have the early Christians resisting participation in practices that torture these animals to death. And as we will discuss in chapter seven, prohibition 1 above may still very much apply to our situation today in which nonhuman animals are tortured and sacrificed in factory farms to the idols of profit and consumerism.

Didn't Jesus Eat Animals and Even Drown Pigs?

The most famous meal of all time—one which has been reenacted billions of times by Christians all over the world—is the Last Supper. Didn't Jesus eat meat, probably lamb, at this meal? And if Jesus did it, then surely then it is OK for us. Stephen H. Webb points out in *A Faith Embracing All Creatures*, however, that none of the biblical stories themselves (or the secondary sources and countless commentaries) give us explicit information about what was served other than bread and wine.

But some believe it isn't mentioned at all because it is perfectly obvious. Jesus was having a Passover meal with his disciples, and, as tradition dictated, there would have been lamb served. But this argument is problematic for at least three reasons. First, Jesus and his disciples often defied the religious laws and customs of his day. (A classic example is the group picking grain in violation of the Sabbath at the end of Mark 2.) Second, it isn't at all clear to Scripture scholars that the Last Supper was, in fact, a Passover meal. Third, even if this was a Passover meal, Webb argues that this is even more evidence that lamb was not at table. After all, if lamb had been present at the very Passover meal during which Jesus defined his ministry, wouldn't he have commented on it as he explained his upcoming death? The symbolism of Jesus's upcoming sacrifice replacing the old Passover sacrifice of the lamb seems too perfect to ignore.

There is little doubt about the fact that Jesus ate and cooked fish, however. He is described doing so at least six times throughout the Gospels, including in Luke 24 when he eats fish apparently as a way of showing that he is not a ghost. Whatever it means to treat animals morally, it must be reconciled with the fact that Jesus ate fish. For, again, Christians start with the conviction that Jesus was not immoral in eating fish.

Andy Alexis-Baker, also writing in A Faith Embracing All Creatures, suggests that one important thing to keep in mind is the fact that Christians should not be expected to imitate every aspect of Jesus's actions. He claims that the question "Didn't Jesus eat fish?" is like asking, "Didn't Jesus go barefoot?" The answer to both questions might be yes, but it doesn't follow that Christians must go barefoot or eat fish simply because Jesus did these things.

The claim being made by animal activists, however, is that those who treat animals unjustly are immoral in so doing. While it is true we aren't called to do everything Jesus did, Christians do seem committed to the idea that the Son of God did not act immorally in eating fish. Indeed, if Jesus ate fish, doesn't it follow that we can eat fish as well?

But in order for this last move to follow, we have to be more specific about why and in what context Jesus ate fish and then compare it with our own reasons and contexts. Jesus lived in the ancient Middle East: a time and a place where protein sources were far less available than in our time. It is reasonable to assume that in order to get a healthy level of protein, Jesus and his disciples had to eat fish. But this is not our situation today. We can get protein in any number of ways (given an overwhelming abundance of soy, lentils, nuts, beans, and other plants with high protein content)— so when we eat fish it has far more to do with the taste and convenience of the food than it is about getting enough protein to stay healthy. Furthermore, modern-day fishing practices have horrible consequences that were not present in Jesus's time. Today's fishing vessels, Alexis-Baker points out, often capture one hundred tons of sea animals per day. There are 90 percent fewer sea creatures today than when industrial commercial fishing began—and this has resulted in everything from serious extinction risks to the crippling of local economies in the developing world, which require smaller-scale fishing to survive. So while it might be moral for someone to eat fish on the small scale required to get enough protein to survive and be healthy, our culture's fish-eating habits hardly qualify as an example of this.

Finally, let us examine Jesus's actions in Mark 5. After driving out a number of unclean spirits (they are collectively called "Legion") from a man, Jesus deposits them into some two thousand pigs nearby who immediately rush into the sea and drown. Jesus shows little regard for the value of pigs. Why couldn't Jesus have simply made the demons vanish into thin air or find some other way to get rid of them? Though there are multiple ways of interpreting this passage, most Scripture scholars see it as a fairly obvious parable of resistance against Rome rather than a historical account of something Jesus actually said or did. The demons' name, Legion, is a dead giveaway here, as it invokes the idea of Roman soldiers. The story is also clear that the placeholder for these soldiers is banished into animals that were considered unclean. The story has nothing to do with what Jesus thought about the value of nonhuman animals; rather, it is a parable about the power Jesus had over the Roman occupiers.

Peter and Paul

Beyond Jesus, authoritative figures like Peter and Paul describe or say things that seem inconsistent with the moral status of nonhuman animals. One story that is often mentioned is Peter's vision in Acts 10. In this story, God speaks to Peter:

> "Get up, Peter; kill and eat." But Peter said, "By no means, Lord; for I have never eaten anything that is profane or unclean." The voice said to him again, a second time, "What God has made clean, you must not call profane." (Acts 10:13–15)

Here it looks like God is explicitly condoning the slaughter and eating of nonhuman animals. But this interpretation makes the same kind of mistake as with the previous passage. The central theological point is made clear later in the chapter when Peter says, "I now realize how true it is that God does not show favoritism but accepts men from every nation who fear him and do what is right." In the next chapter of Acts, when Peter is asked to explain why he is hanging out and eating with the unclean Gentiles, Peter describes this vision as his reason. His vision is recalled as a theological point about the proper relationship between Christians and Gentiles, not to justify the slaughter and eating of nonhuman animals.

But chapter nine of Paul's First Letter to the Corinthians might present us with a more difficult problem:

> For it is written in the law of Moses, "You shall not muzzle an ox while it is treading out the grain." Is it for oxen that God is concerned? Or does he not speak entirely for our sake? It was indeed written for our sake, for whoever ploughs should plough in hope and whoever threshes should thresh in hope of a share in the crop. (1 Corinthians 9:9–10)

Paul seems to be telling us that, while some divine rules or commands seem to imply the independent moral status of nonhuman animals, the real good is ultimately for human beings. But Paul, of course, is not Jesus. He was a man of classical Greek culture who had problematic views not only about nonhuman animals but also about women—even telling them that they could not speak in Church and that they must be submissive to their husbands. Not everything Paul says in his letters is inspired by God, especially when it conflicts with what Jesus tells us:

Therefore I tell you, do not worry about your life, what you will eat or what you will drink, or about your body, what you will wear. Is not life more than food, and the body more than clothing? Look at the birds of the air; they neither sow nor reap nor gather into barns, and yet your heavenly Father feeds them. Are you not of more value than they? And can any of you by worrying add a single hour to your span of life? (Matthew 6:25–27)

And:

Are not five sparrows sold for two pennies? Yet not one of them is forgotten in God's sight. But even the hairs of your head are all counted. Do not be afraid; you are of more value than many sparrows. (Luke 12:6–7)

Humans are worth more than many sparrows, but Jesus tells us that God cares about the sparrows too. Does God care for animals? Though Paul appears to say no, Jesus says yes. Christians must go with Jesus on this one.

Ruling over Nonhuman Animals?

Recall from chapter two that both Peter Singer and Lynn White, Jr., are very critical of the theological concept of humans ruling or having dominion over nonhuman animals. Indeed, what you think about what God intended with this idea can color what you think about many of the other topics we discussed in this chapter. If you think of rule or dominion as domination—where, say, humans were intended by God simply to use nonhuman animals however we see fit—then it becomes easier to interpret many of the passages above in a way that is unfriendly to nonhuman animals.

But whatever God meant by rule or dominion, it is apparently consistent with something else presented a few lines later: Nonhuman animals are created to be the companions—and not the food—of human beings. David Clough has a compelling explanation of this kind of dominion. He says that part of what it means for human beings to be made in the image of God is that we are set up as the creatures best able to take a "God's eye view of creation and make judgments about how it should appropriately be ordered." This kind of rule or dominion has been revealed to us primarily in the person of Jesus Christ who interpreted his Lordship, not as domination, but as servanthood. If Clough is correct, and I believe he is, we are called to be like Jesus and use our dominion to serve and protect the most vulnerable. This includes vulnerable nonhuman animals. With Christ as our guide, human dominion over creation must be about self-sacrificial love—not consumerist exploitation.

Whatever God permitted in light of human violence and sin, God's intent was a human race that did not eat nonhuman animals—a peaceful kingdom in which they are companions rather than food. We are told by the prophets not only that God does not want animal sacrifices, but that this peaceful kingdom between humans and animals is coming. There are passages in Scripture that are ambiguous about nonhuman animals, no question about it. These must be confronted openly and honestly. But when we read them through the lens of the peaceful servant-lordship of Jesus it becomes clear that we should read them in ways that see nonhuman animals as part of the peaceful kingdom toward which all Christians are striving. Indeed, the dominion

God gives us brings with it both great power and great responsibility in this regard.

If you are thinking that there are still important questions to ask about nonhuman animals, you are certainly correct. The Bible does not give us all the answers to every single question— particularly the new questions raised by technologies that were unimaginable at the time the Bible was written. In the next chapter we will move to explore the postbiblical Christian tradition on nonhuman animals, and particularly the witness and wisdom of holy people who were clearly close to God.

QUESTIONS FOR DISCUSSION

1. Do you think the sixth day of creation shows that humans were created to be vegetarian? How does this connect with God's permission to eat animals in Genesis 9? How, if at all, is sin involved in this apparent shift?

2. What aspects of the Jewish law did the early Christians decide to keep? How are they related to nonhuman animals? Do they have any relevance for us today?

3. How should Christians think about the peaceful kingdom that once existed in Eden and will come to be at the end of time? Do we have a responsibility to witness to God's will being "done on earth as it is in heaven"?

4. Is it possible to have dominion over nonhuman animals and still see them as our companions rather than our food? How much should a Christian understanding of dominion or authority be different from a secular understanding?

SUGGESTIONS FOR FURTHER READING

"The Chief End of All Flesh" by John Berkman and Stanley Hauerwas, in *Theology Today*, July 1992

A Faith Embracing All Creatures: Addressing Commonly Asked Questions about Christian Care for Animals edited by Andy Alexis-Baker and Tripp York (especially chapters three, five, and six)

"How to Respect Other Animals" by David Clough, in *Christian Ethics Engages Peter Singer* (a paper given at conference at University of Oxford Conference, May 2011)

Peter Singer and Christian Ethics by Charles C. Camosy

Why Animal Suffering Matters: Philosophy, Theology, and Practical Ethics by Andrew Linzey

CHAPTER FIVE

SAINTS AND OTHER GREAT CHRISTIAN FIGURES

THE BIBLE FORMS THE FOUNDATION for a Christian's understanding of the moral life. And as we saw in the previous chapter, it offers much for us to think about with regard to nonhuman animals. But because the Bible does not speak to every topic (especially issues of modern technology), and because there are different reasonable ways to interpret what the Bible says, hundreds of millions of Christians look for insight from the wisdom of God as it continues to inspire the Church throughout history, up until the present moment. In fact, we can have all the abstract conclusions and principles we want, but it is still very difficult to act on them without the examples of real people to inspire us with their example and lead the way. In this chapter, we will see Christian concern for animals on display in everything from condemnation of Roman gladiatorial games to Francis of Assisi's sermons to C.S. Lewis's books.

It may take some readers by surprise to learn that many Christians throughout the centuries have had deep concern for nonhuman animals. Holly Roberts has shown in her book *Vegetarian Christian Saints* that many dozens of these people have been recognized as some of the holiest people in the tradition.

Indeed, this recognition merely continues the biblical tradition in which kindness to animals was understood as an important mark of holiness. Jacob and David, for instance, were considered holy based in part on how they cared for other animals. Also, Rebecca was thought to be an appropriate wife for Isaac because of her kindness to animals, and the Talmud specifically states that Moses was chosen for his leadership role because of his skill in caring for animals.

The Early Christians

Christian vegetarianism existed from the very beginning. Some of the earliest people to believe in Jesus Christ, often called the Ebionites, practiced rather strict vegetarianism. But these were likely exceptional communities living apart from the general population. All early Christians, of course, lived under the rule of the Roman Empire, and one of the key things that Roman rule brought with it was a near-obsession with gladiatorial games and spectacles. These games basically had the role that American and European football currently have our Western world. But despite this nearly essential role in the social life of a Roman-ruled area, many important leaders of the early Church sharply criticized the violence present in the games and even claimed that authentic Christians should refrain from attending.

One can understand why early Christian leaders made such decrees, given the horrific and cruel violence directed at gladiators, criminals, and prisoners, but early Church leaders also had deep concern for nonhuman animals at the games. These animals were denied food for days and then made to fight both human beings and each other—all for the pleasure of the crowd. Historian Thomas Wiedermann notes that early Christian leaders were concerned about the effect that witnessing the violence would have on spectators. In the view of Tertullian, for instance, repeated watching of exotic wild animals from around the empire fighting each other to death turned the crowd into "savages." Gregory of Nazianzen considered both "men killing one another" and "the slaughter of wild beasts" to be on the same list of problems with the games themselves. Basil the Great criticized the "wealthy men" who, for "secular honor" make men fight wild beasts.

But about what, precisely, were these great Church leaders worried? Consider that it was not unheard of to have over ten thousand nonhuman animals killed during a single celebration season: from tigers, to elephants, to pythons, to bears, to crocodiles. Would they have been similarly concerned about their fellow Christians watching, say, ten thousand trees get hacked to death? Of course not. As we saw with the case of Michael Vick in chapter one, it was precisely the horrific harm being inflicted on the during the games nonhuman animals which caused those who witnessed thousands of their vicious and violent deaths to become savages.

It was also part of an early Christian worldview that nonhuman animals could at least sense, and perhaps even understand, goodness and holiness. Fordham University's eminent early Church historian Maureen Tilley explains that we can see this especially in the stories of the martyrs. In two separate incidents, though saints Paul and Thecla were thrown to the lions to be eaten, the lions recognized their holiness and refused to harm them. Other stories include a bear brought to torture some Christian prisoners, but who refused to come out of its cage; and a boar who not only refused to attack Christians, but who turned against the

Romans instead. When some animals could not prevent Christian martyrdom, they could at least reverence the bodies of the martyrs: hence the amazing stories of martyrs' bodies being returned home by dolphins and other animals for proper burial and veneration.

Tilley also recalls that nonhuman animals and early Christian holy persons had close relationships, especially in the desert. She describes stories of hyenas bringing their cubs for monks to heal, monks calling on snakes to guard their cells, and crocodiles ferrying monks across rivers. Hundreds of years before Francis of Assisi preached to the birds, we learn of monks preaching to some violent nonhuman animals. Inspired by their words, the animals ceased ravaging the countryside. Tilley argues that the common Christian belief of the day would have been that these nonhuman animals knew exactly what they were doing and with whom they were dealing. Thus they acted appropriately in the presence of a holy person of God.

The early Orthodox Christian churches of the East did an even better job of acknowledging the biblically supported moral value of nonhuman animals than Catholics did in the West. John Chrysostom and Basil the Great, for example, appear to be much friendlier to nonhuman animals than their counterparts in the Western Church. Though one could point to many other similar examples from these Eastern churches, the third-century martyr St. Mamas of Paphlagonia is worth highlighting because he is still invoked today by various Orthodox Christians in their prayers for nonhuman animals.

Albert the Great, Thomas Aquinas, and Francis of Assisi

The period after the fall of Rome is sometimes referred to as the Dark Ages. The implication is that the people of this time lived in ignorance until the secular Enlightenment came about in the 1500s. But only those who are unfamiliar with the holy and brilliant Christians of this era could possibly think such a thing; some of the greatest saints and thinkers of the Christian Church lived and taught during this time. There are literally dozens of figures we could feature in this section, but space allows me to briefly consider only the following wonderful figures.

Albert the Great is so titled in part because of his great knowledge and learning. In addition to being a bishop and Dominican friar, Albert was known for harmonizing religion, philosophy, and science. A virtual encyclopedia of knowledge, he was an expert of all the writings of Aristotle and he put his theological and philosophical insights in conversation with all the natural sciences of his day—everything from botany to chemistry to zoology. In addition to everything else, Albert was the most important zoologist of the Middle Ages, and he studied nonhuman animals in painstaking detail. Some of his insights (particularly about animal reproductive systems) would not be eclipsed for several hundred years.

Albert was an internationally famous professor at the best school of his time, the University of Paris. It was here that Albert mentored a brilliant student named Thomas Aquinas: a man who would go on to become arguably the greatest thinker in the history of the Christian Church. Remarkably, despite being trained by Albert, Thomas has very little to say about nonhuman animals. But John Berkman, a moral theologian and student of Thomas's works, points out that if one is willing to dig around a bit, his thinking actually supports a rather sophisticated view of nonhuman animals. We should understand animals, says

Berkman, in the context of Thomas's larger picture of the entire physical universe as ordered toward its own perfection. Each living creature manifests the goodness of God by living according to its own nature and way of flourishing. For Thomas, the highest good after God is not the good of human beings, but the good of the order of the whole universe. When looking at the universe as a whole, differences between human and nonhuman animals become even less stark because—as we saw above—human beings do not have a particularly high slot in the hierarchy of creation. We are actually ranked by Thomas as the lowest of creatures with rational natures.

Berkman also points out that, for Thomas, nonhuman animals share with human animals a spiritual reality or soul. He didn't think that the nonhuman animal soul was rational, but even if he is correct about this (and we will explore this question more in chapter nine), it is remarkable how much sophisticated behavior Thomas thought beings with a nonrational soul could perform. This animal soul can know and feel via emotion and thus could feel fear, hate, or experience joy or anger. Furthermore, there are a host of activities which human and nonhuman animals perform "without rationality" as Thomas understood the term. In addition to learning certain motor skills, memorizing information for a test, or even making a sandwich, Berkman and many other Thomistic thinkers believe that even Thomas thought animals have a reason for doing what they do. And if an animal has a reason for doing what it does, then how far are we away from concluding that this animal has self-awareness?

Let us conclude this discussion on the Middle Ages with the great St. Francis of Assisi and his love and concern for nonhuman animals. Along with being the most beloved saint in the Christian tradition, Francis is the patron saint of nonhuman animals. Beyond the famous stories of him preaching to (and otherwise interacting with) many kinds of animals, the order he founded— the Franciscans—has maintained this special concern for animals throughout the centuries. (In some ways, Franciscan Media publishing this book is just another example of this tradition.) Even today, the Catholic feast day celebrating the life of St. Francis is also the day on which Catholics around the world bring their animals to Church to have them blessed. On his World Day of Peace address in 1990, Pope John Paul II invoked St. Francis in the following way:

> Saint Francis invited all of creation—animals, plants, natural forces, even Brother Sun and Sister Moon—to give honour and praise to the Lord.... It is my hope that the inspiration of Saint Francis will help us to keep ever alive a sense of "fraternity" with all those good and beautiful things which Almighty God has created. And may he remind us of our serious obligation to respect and watch over them with care.[1]

William Wilberforce, C.S. Lewis, and J.R.R. Tolkien
We finish this chapter by considering three great Christian figures from the nineteenth and twentieth centuries. Though he is best known for his dramatic and inspiring fight to ban the English slave trade, the evangelical Christian hero William Wilberforce did far more than this. He applied his biblically inspired nonviolent concern for the most vulnerable, not only to humans, but to nonhuman animals as well. Wilberforce led the fight to outlaw bullbaiting in Britain and was a founding member of the Royal

Society for the Prevention of Cruelty to Animals. Beyond his political work to curb violence directed at nonhuman animals, we also have several stories of Wilberforce personally confronting such violence. Upon seeing a horse being beaten by its would-be rider, for instance, Wilberforce reportedly stopped his own horse and proceeded to publicly berate the animal abuser for his immoral behavior.

Anyone familiar with the major characters in *The Chronicles of Narnia* series might be able to guess that C.S. Lewis had a deep love for nonhuman animals. An orthodox Anglican Christian who was interested in providing a public and rational defense of his faith, Lewis was particularly bothered by the vast amount of suffering in a world created by a loving God. While he was of course concerned about the suffering of human beings, he also gave an incredible amount of attention to the suffering of nonhuman animals. This concern was expressed in his famous essay "On the Pains of Animals," in a chapter on animal suffering in his classic work *The Problem of Pain,* and in an entire book on animal experimentation he called simply *Vivisection.* As a teenager, Lewis had rejected his Christian upbringing in favor of atheism. But on the basis of conversations and arguments with his devout Roman Catholic friend and fellow University of Oxford professor J.R.R. Tolkien, C.S. Lewis returned to his faith. Lewis and Tolkien met weekly in an Oxford pub called The Eagle and Child and the conversations between them focused on, among other things, their mutual love of nonhuman animals.

Upon reflection, it is easy to see that J.R.R. Tolkien had a deep love and concern for the nonhuman. After all, Tolkien's world of Middle-earth was explicitly designed to draw our attention outside of our human selves. His two major story lines focus on the heroic adventures of nonhuman persons called Hobbits. Perhaps the most powerful characters in his books are the great eagles: creatures who are able not only to speak and interact as persons, but who time and time again come to the rescue when things seem most grim. Tolkien even personalizes trees in the form of Ents, shepherds of the forest, who also play an important heroic role. Perhaps even more telling than descriptions of individuals, however, is the relationship Tolkien envisions between nonhuman animals and the heroes of his stories. Gandalf and Samwise Gamgee, for instance, consider their steeds (Shadowfax and Bill) to be more like friends than mere vehicles to get from A to B. Tolkien describes Radagast the Brown—a "good and honest wizard"—as living in the woods and having deep and close relationships with nonhuman animals. The close relationship that Tolkien envisions between humans and nonhumans is personified in the character of Beorn, champion of the Battle of Five Armies, who shape-shifts between the form of a human and the form of a bear.

Despite pressure from our natural human tendency to become self-obsessed speciesists, along with the influence of the secular Enlightenment, biblical concern for nonhuman animals has remained an important part of our Christian tradition. From the very earliest Christians to the great Christian writers of the twentieth century, this concern was passed on to the next generation of believers. In this next chapter, however, we will look specifically at how this concern has arrived to us today through the current teaching and views of the Church.

Questions for Discussion

1. Christians stood against cruelty against nonhuman animals in the Roman games. What practices might Christians stand against today using similar reasoning?

2. Is kindness to nonhuman animals a sign of holiness? Is cruelty to such animals a sign of something else?

3. Several holy people in the Christian tradition preached to nonhuman animals. What are we to make of this today? Do you think animals can sense goodness and holiness (or their opposite) in human beings?

4. William Wilberforce saw his work to end slavery and to end cruel practices toward nonhuman animals as connected. Do you agree?

5. What do you make of the concern that C.S. Lewis and J.R.R. Tolkien had for animals? Have Christians lost that concern in the twenty-first century?

Suggestions for Future Reading

The Ebionites and Jewish Christianity by Gregory Finley

Emperors and Gladiators by Thomas Wiedemann

Francis of Assisi: Performing the Gospel of Life by Lawrence S. Cunningham

"Martyrs, Monks, Insects and Animals" by Maureen Tilley, in *The Medieval World of Nature: A Book of Essays,* edited by Joyce E. Salisbury

The Problem of Pain and *Vivisection* by C.S. Lewis

Questions Concerning Aristotle's On Animals by Albert the Great

Vegetarian Christian Saints by Holly H. Roberts

William Wilberforce: A Biography by Stephen Tomkins

CHAPTER SIX

CONTEMPORARY TEACHINGS
AND VIEWS

IN THE PREVIOUS TWO CHAPTERS we focused on sources in our Christian tradition that discussed the moral status and treatment of nonhuman animals. But both the Christian Bible and the broader Christian tradition do not always have an obvious message and sometimes require interpretation. This is especially true on controversial issues like sexuality, divorce, war, and, yes, our topic in this book. In this chapter we will begin by exploring the interpretation and teaching of the Roman Catholic Church. I write this book as a Catholic Christian, so it is with this body of teaching that I find myself in conversation but, as with other parts of this book, I urge readers who do not have this teaching as part of their tradition to keep an open mind. After all, as long as you are a person of good will and have an open mind, these ideas are proposed for your consideration as well.

The Current Teaching of the Church

On some issues we saw that the witness of the Bible and the saints on nonhuman animals speaks for itself, but others require further interpretation and reflection. Let's recall some of the teachings of the Church on these matters that we have already encountered. Highlighting the first chapter of Genesis as the basis for its position, we saw that the *Catechism of the Catholic Church* (337–338) claims that "the whole of creation" has an inner nature and value and that God made all creatures "interdependent." Also recall the remarkable passage from the *Catechism* (703) which, again citing Scripture, explains that the "Word of God and his Breath are at the origin of the being and life of every creature." These teachings are consistent with the ideas we read about in the *Compendium of the Social Doctrine of the Church*, including the claim (citing Romans 8) that all of creation participates in the redemption of Jesus Christ.

But these teachings are more about creation broadly speaking than about nonhuman animals in particular. One reason for this is, despite the fact that ecological and environmental issues have been front and center in the Catholic Church for the better part of a decade, the subject of nonhuman animals hasn't taken off in the same way. Frankly, the Church just hasn't had much to say about it. But let's take a careful look at the one place in the *Catechism* (2415–2418) where it is directly addressed:

> [D]ominion over inanimate and other living beings granted by the Creator is not absolute; it is limited by concern for the quality of life of his neighbor, including generations to come; it requires a religious respect for the integrity of creation.
>
> Animals are God's creatures. He surrounds them with his providential care. By their mere existence they bless him and give him glory. Thus men owe them kindness. We should recall the gentleness with which saints like St. Francis of Assisi or St. Philip Neri treated animals.

> God entrusted animals to the stewardship of those whom
> he created in his own image. Hence it is legitimate to use
> animals for food and clothing. They may be domesticated to
> help man in his work and leisure....
>
> It is contrary to human dignity to cause animals to suffer
> or die needlessly.[2]

Let's look very carefully at this teaching and try to unpack it.
First, we see that the Church agrees with and promotes the biblical
teaching of Jesus that God cares about nonhuman animals. But
then, interestingly, we see that it is precisely because of God's
providential care that we human beings owe nonhuman animals
kindness. This is not merely a suggestion, or an extra thing that
might be nice to do. Very strong language is used; indeed, it is the
language of justice. We *owe* animals kindness. And, just to clear
up any doubt about what is being proposed here, the Church asks
us to follow the example of the saints who put this kindness into
practice.

But as with the broader Christian tradition, there are compli-
cating factors and tensions even with this relatively brief teaching.
The *Catechism* rightly points out that God has entrusted human
beings with the care and stewardship of nonhuman animals, but
this apparently goes beyond caring for the well-being of such
animals. We are also told that they may be used for food and
clothing and may be domesticated for help with work or leisure.

Is this "game over" for a Catholic understanding of the moral
status and treatment of nonhuman animals? After all, most other
animal-friendly traditions and movements prohibit this kind of
behavior. Before making sweeping conclusions, let's take another
look at the final line from the above passage. It turns out to be

rather important that the *Catechism of the Catholic Church* prohibits causing nonhuman animals to "suffer or die needlessly." This puts the previous line into an important context. Yes, the Church teaches that human beings may use nonhuman animals for food and clothing, but we may not cause them to suffer or die unless we need to. This is a strikingly clear and demanding view. As we will see in the next chapter, most of our use of nonhuman animals for food and clothing causes them to suffer and die— often in horrific ways. Do we actually *need* to use such animals for food and clothing?

The Popes on Animals

It is anything but shocking that the previous two popes have expressed views that are consistent with the *Catechism*. Everyone who knows Benedict XVI well, for instance, is aware that he is a huge animal lover and even had to be reminded that he could not take in stray cats from the surrounding Roman streets. PETA took advantage of this fact and promoted his words in their advertisements. One flier that got a lot of public attention focused on his response to a question asked of him by German journalist Peter Seewald not long before he became pope when he was in charge of safeguarding Catholic doctrine. Seewald asked, "Are we allowed to make use of animals, and even to eat them?" His response would eventually become the basis of a PETA advertisement:

> That is a very serious question. At any rate, we can see that they are given into our care, that we cannot just do whatever we want with them. Animals, too, are God's creatures.... Certainly, a sort of industrial use of creatures, so that geese are fed in such a way as to produce as large a liver

as possible, or hens live so packed together that they become just caricatures of birds, this degrading of living creatures to a commodity seems to me in fact to contradict the relationship of mutuality that comes across in the Bible.[3]

We have already seen that in his encyclical *Caritas in Veritate* Pope Benedict exhorts all of humanity to be faithful to what he claims is a "covenant" between humans and the rest of creation. And it seems clear that Benedict's view of nonhuman animals comes out of this very strong concern for everything that God has made. He will go down in history as the first "Green Pope" in light of his repeated and energetic efforts to connect concern for creation with the Church's broader teachings. Indeed, this theme was present in Benedict's first homily as pope in which he said that the "external deserts" in the world are growing because the "internal deserts" in human beings have become so large.

This was not mere talk from the pope. Under Benedict's leadership, the Vatican became the world's first carbon-neutral country by offsetting its emissions though renewable energies and carbon credits. Benedict also led on the topic of renewable energy by putting thousands of solar panels on various Vatican buildings and in the process reducing carbon dioxide emissions by about 225 tons. This project even won the Euro Solar Prize in 2008 from the (secular) European Association for Renewable Energy.

The teachings of John Paul II also had an important environmental focus—and also impacted his view of nonhuman animals. In his encyclical *Sollicitudo Rei Socialis* John Paul said that authentic human development "imposes limits on the use of the natural world" such that we are not free to "use and misuse" creation as we see fit.[4] In 2000, he addressed European farmers and asked them to resist the temptations of productivity and profit that work against our respect for nature. For when we become tyrants and not custodians, John Paul warned, the earth will eventually rebel against us.

This general thinking was then applied specifically to how we treat nonhuman animals. On the eight hundredth anniversary of the death of St. Francis, patron saint of animals, John Paul II said, "It is necessary and urgent that with the example of the little poor man from Assisi, one decides to abandon unadvisable forms of domination, the locking up of all creatures." The pope also built on the fact that nonhuman animals have "the breath of life" by claiming during one papal audience that nonhuman animals "have souls" and that we "love and feel solidarity with our smaller brethren."

It is interesting and a source of hope that Pope Francis has taken the name of the Christian saint most associated with concern for nonhuman animals. In addition to emphasizing the need to protect "all of God's creatures" in his very first homily, Francis also recently broke protocol by insisting that the canine helper of a sight-impaired journalist be allowed into the hall to greet him. The pope blessed not only the journalist, but gave a "special blessing for your dog, too." Look for Pope Francis to continue, and perhaps even expand, the growing tradition of papal concern for animals.

A Soft or Sentimental Point of View?

Let's be honest about something. Concern for nonhuman animals, especially in the political culture of the United States, has a reputation. Generally, it is associated with the sentimental views of the far left. When someone mentions animal rights, for instance, many people associate this movement with PETA and Hollywood and their "soft and fuzzy" approaches to these issues. Some Catholics I know even try to dismiss my animal-friendly religious views as a kind of post–Vatican II liberalism—just another example of the Church going down the soft and sentimental path of surrender to the ideas of the modern world, ungrounded in the broad Catholic tradition.

But as we've already seen above, this couldn't be more wrong. While it is true that some leaders in the secular animal rights movement have a soft or sentimental approach, this is not the Catholic approach to nonhuman animals. Disciplining our appetites so that we do not participate in injustice is anything but soft. Indeed, it is at the heart of what it means to be Catholic. We see this quite clearly when it comes to the Church's expectations, for instance, with regard to other issues such as giving to the poor, fasting, and chastity. We are expected to do the hard work involved in resisting the allure of sexual desire, hunger, and consumerism. Resisting our culture's addiction to unjust use of nonhuman animals for food and clothing—like resisting other kinds of injustice—requires countercultural commitment, determination, and strength.

Indeed, for all of its essential and important reforms, one could argue that the aftermath of Second Vatican Council took us in a questionably speciesist direction by focusing almost exclusively on the dignity of the human person. I was recently saddened to find that if you search for *animal* in *Gaudium et Spes* (Vatican II's lengthy document explaining its understanding of the Church in the Modern World) you will find exactly zero entries. John Berkman has pointed out that Catholic theology after the Council pretty much ignored moral concern for nonhuman animals. Ironically, pre–Vatican II moral theology, for all its weaknesses, actually had extended consideration of the moral status and treatment of nonhuman animals.

So, no, Christian concern for nonhuman animals is not a turn to a soft or sentimental approach. Instead, it follows from the best of the Christian tradition, holistically considered, and places strict demands on our behavior—something with which authentic Christians should already be familiar in other areas of life. But don't take my word for it; consider the following voices who are speaking out in defense of the moral status and treatment of nonhuman animals.

A Politically Diverse Movement

Admittedly, the most public voices on nonhuman animals do not seem politically diverse. From PETA promoting naked photo spreads of Hollywood heartthrobs speaking out against fur to Bill Clinton's going vegan, the loudest and most promoted voices in the public conversation are from the left. But what if I told you that George W. Bush's speechwriter, Matthew Scully, wrote an important and popular book called *Dominion* which argued that conservatives should strongly consider the moral status and treatment of nonhuman animals? This book, laudably, pulls no punches. Scully calls our current treatment of nonhuman animals "crimes against nature"—and boldly says that the only thing worse than the cruelty we directly perpetuate against nonhuman animals comes when we delegate another person to do the dirty work for us because we are uncomfortable being part of the cruel process ourselves. The way we justify our practices, says Scully, requires a disconnected arrogance that reveals most human beings as terrible stewards of God's creation. Our decisions about how to treat nonhuman animals reveal our character and our capacity for empathy and faithful stewardship. We have a duty to treat these animals with kindness, he argues, not because they are our equals, but in a sense because they are *not* our equals. Christians, as we learned in the very first chapter, have a special duty to serve the most vulnerable. Scully rightly points out that both liberals and conservatives have utterly failed in this solemn duty when it comes to nonhuman animals.

And Scully is not alone. A senior fellow at the Ethics and Public Policy Center, and a regular writer for publications such as *First Things, The Weekly Standard,* and *The Wall Street Journal,* Mary Eberstadt is certainly well-known and respected in conservative circles. She actually wrote an article for *First Things* called "The Vindication of *Humanae Vitae*" and argued that contraception has hurt the flourishing of women. Her readers must have been surprised, therefore, when she wrote a very different article for *First Things* titled "Pro-Animal, Pro-Life." Here Eberstadt attempts to link concern for nonhuman animals with moral concern for our prenatal children and abortion. She notes that most conservatives have relished bashing vegetarianism for decades, but Eberstadt pushes back by arguing that it is not easily dismissed from either an intellectual or moral point of view. She notes that confusion in most discussions about abortion is similar to the confusion in most discussions about nonhuman animals. Contrary to what both most animal-rights liberals and pro-life conservatives believe, she says, clear-headed thinking (when unclouded by simplistic political ideology) reveals that it is quite easy to connect the dots between moral concern for nonhuman animals and for our prenatal children.

Eberstadt also argues that developing a concern for nonhuman animals is much easier for young people, not least because their habits and practices can be changed more easily. Many children, for instance, react with sickness and revulsion when they learn for the first time that they are "eating the animals they just petted on the farm." We have been socialized to accept eating animals, but the example of the little children reacting this way, says Eberstadt, should make us think twice.

Finally, consider Duke University's Stanley Hauerwas—a man who was proclaimed America's best theologian by *Time* magazine in part because of his well-known attempts to consistently promote a nonviolent defense of life. Unlike the overwhelming majority of his colleagues, he has applied his concern for nonviolence to nonhuman animals in a way that no one could dismiss as the view of a sentimental liberal. He believes the Bible reveals that the main difference between human and nonhuman animals is in the purpose given to each group by God. Human dominion over creation means that our job is to "name" the animals by telling them who they are as creatures known and cared for by God. This, says Hauerwas, should not be described in the secular language of animal rights—which implies the very consumerist, secular Enlightenment model that caused humans to see nonhuman animals merely as a means to our ends in the first place. Unlike the sentimental views of some who argue for animal rights, Hauwerwas argues that humans are indeed meant to rule and have dominion over nonhuman animals. But how we are to rule over them should be modeled on how Jesus, the Prince of Peace, rules over us. His lordship involves a radical suspicion of violence and a commitment to servant leadership. And if Christ's dominion over us does not imply domination, but rather nonviolence and service, then the same should be true of our dominion over nonhuman animals.

Hauerwas was not content to let his theoretical views simply linger in the seminar rooms of Duke's ivory towers. These views have practical implications for how all of us are called to live our lives. Indeed, he boldly concludes that Christians may be called to give up meat-eating entirely if they want to be faithful to what the Prince of Peace demands of us. These demands transcend the secular and American liberal and conservative categories that dominate our public discussion of these matters. Christians should put aside the idolatry of Americanism and instead take a hard look at whether our current habits and practices can be justified from the perspective of our ancient tradition. The next three chapters will explore our habits and practices in some detail. How should Christians think about hunting animals or owning pets? What about benefiting from medical research on animals? And, of course, we have already asked about eating meat in this book multiple times. But in part because we do it so much, the topic of meat-eating deserves especially careful consideration. And we begin our exploration of this topic by focusing on factory farming.

QUESTIONS FOR DISCUSSION

1. What do you think of Catholic teaching on nonhuman animals? Are animals owed kindness from us? Is it ever acceptable to cause nonhuman animals to suffer and die needlessly?

2. Do you think Catholic teaching on nonhuman animals is grounded in the Bible and broader Christian tradition? Why or why not?

3. Were you surprised that Pope Benedict XVI and Pope John Paul II had the views they did on nonhuman animals?

4. Can one be a vegetarian or activist in favor of the moral status and treatment of nonhuman animals and also be a conservative?

5. Are human beings strong enough to change their current habits and practices if they are convinced that they violate their Christian commitments? Is this easier for younger people or older people?

SUGGESTIONS FOR FURTHER READING

Catechism of the Catholic Church (especially 2415–2418)

"The Chief End of All Flesh" by John Berkman and Stanley Hauerwas, in *Theology Today,* July 1992

Dominion: The Power of Man, the Suffering of Animals, and the Call to Mercy by Matthew Scully

God and the World: A Conversation with Peter Seewald by Cardinal Joseph Ratzinger

Peter Singer and Christian Ethics by Charles C. Camosy

"Pro-Animal, Pro-Life" by Mary Eberstadt, in *First Things* June/July 2009

CHAPTER SEVEN

FACTORY FARMING

SHOULD CHRISTIANS EAT MEAT? PERHAPS you've had this question in the back of your mind several times already while reading this book. Before we turn to this important question, however, we must first explore and understand precisely how we get the meat we eat. Especially given the increased movement of people into urban areas, we are now more disconnected from nonhuman animals (and how our food gets to our plates) than at any point in human history. For many of us our most direct contact with animals is when we eat them. A few may have some vague idea that these animals may have not been treated very well, but our culture of eating is so disconnected from the process by which we get our meat that we almost never have to think about this. Even the words we use (like *pork* instead of *pig* and *beef* instead of *cow*) are designed to disconnect us from the fact that we are eating the flesh of a nonhuman animal.

Some argue that modern-day factory farms are not nearly as bad as some activists claim. Indeed, some will argue that even the term "factory farm" itself is an emotionally loaded word meant to manipulate people into turning against decent companies which not only treat nonhuman animals well (something that is necessary, they say, in order for them to turn a profit) but who deliver necessary and healthy protein at an affordable price. This is a special concern for the poor, who might not be able to get protein any other way.

Later we will explore whether those in poverty need factory-farmed meat to get enough protein affordably, but here and now we will directly challenge the view that factory farms treat nonhuman animals well. Over the past fifty years or so, the meat industry has transformed from many small and independent farms to a few and very large farms which operate essentially as huge animal factories. Instead of seeing nonhuman animals as intrinsically valuable, factory farms treat them as mere products. In the language of the business, they are valuable as "protein units" and their welfare and flourishing is a concern only insofar as the corporation who owns them can sell these protein units to make a profit. We will see that the process by which businesses determine the most cost-effective way to raise protein units is so complex that it now requires massive amounts of computing power. These corporations have a financial interest, of course, in making sure the public and government believe that they treat nonhuman animals well, and they understandably lobby the government hard at both the state and federal levels to keep their production methods secret. As I write this chapter, there are bills pending in multiple states that would ban even taking a photograph or video of the process by which factory farms produce protein units.

Perhaps you are skeptical about descriptions of factory farms, especially when they come from organizations that are obviously biased. I can understand this skepticism. That is why the descriptions of factory farming in this chapter will come primarily from two unbiased sources. The first is the 2008 Pew Report from its Commission on Industrial Farm Animals Protection, which was produced in concert with the Johns Hopkins Bloomberg School of Public Health. Members of this group included several people involved in the food industry, including the chairman of the commission, John Carlin, who is a former dairy farmer. This group conducted eleven meetings over two years, including meetings in every major region of the United States. Two public hearings were held where more than 175 people spoke directly to the commission. The commission visited industrial animal farms in Iowa, California, North Carolina, Arkansas, and Colorado. In addition, the commission visited a teaching facility at Iowa State University to learn more about the latest in industrial animal production. All testimony and reports can be found on its website: http://www. ncifap.org/.

The second major source of information is from the publications of those who work in the animal agriculture industry: journals like *Poultry Science*, *The Veterinary Record*, *Avian Advice*, and the *World Poultry Science Journal*. In addition, we will get important information from an article written by the chief information officer of an industrial chicken farm about the kind of technology necessary to run a modern-day factory farm. In what follows, I focus mainly on how we get chicken meat and pig meat from these farms, but I could have just as easily focused on how we get eggs, milk, or cow meat. Please see the suggestions for further reading if you are interested in more information.

Nonhuman Animals in Factory Farms

Whenever I consider how to write or teach about factory farms, I feel conflicted about how to describe their treatment of nonhuman animals. On the one hand, I want my readers and students to be able to trust me to be fair, and some of the descriptions that follow below might seem like emotional manipulation. But on the other hand, we cannot honestly address a serious and complex problem without directly confronting and understanding the specifics in all their relevant detail. This is true whether we are talking about the genocide in Rwanda, the 1.2 million abortions every year in the United States, or the factory farming of nonhuman animals. In what follows I do my best to be honest and direct without being emotionally manipulative. For many, this will make for uncomfortable reading. Indeed, some family members and close friends have told me, "Charlie, I just can't read your stuff on animals because I know that it will force me to change." But can any of us, especially if we are Christians, really take this approach when it comes to deciding whether or not we are participating in serious violence and injustice? Are we justified in simply choosing to ignore the uncomfortable facts of factory farming merely because we would prefer to continue our comfortable, ignorant way of life?

The overwhelming majority of the meat we eat comes from factory farms. Indeed, if it does not have a specific label like "free range"—and sometimes even if does—or come directly from a small farm it is almost certainly from a factory farm. To meet the overwhelming demand for meat in the developed West, factory farms produce and slaughter well over fifty billion nonhuman animals each year. In the interest of maximizing protein units per square foot, factory farms confine these animals into spaces that so severely restrict their movement and other behaviors that they are often unable to walk or even turn around. No federal regulations protect them before they are slaughtered; even the Humane Methods of Slaughter Act does not protect birds, and these animals make up more than 95 percent of the land animals killed for food in the United States.

Chickens

The life of a chicken in a factory farm is miserable, short, and often full of pain. There are more than one hundred million chickens slaughtered each week in the United States, and they spend most of their lives in almost complete darkness in about half a square foot of living space. If they are fortunate enough to have the freedom to move about on the ground (many live tightly confined in stacked wire cages and are pelted with excrement from chickens in the cages above them), the floor is generally covered with excrement. The ammonia created by the excrement is so thick that, in addition to giving them chronic respiratory disease, it causes some chickens to go blind. In the interest of maximizing protein units produced per bird, factory farms have bred them so quickly and with breasts so large that it hurts them even to stand up. They therefore spend much of their time sitting in excrement and develop breast blisters.

As you might imagine, this kind of existence causes a lot of stress and in such close quarters leads the birds to fight with each other—usually by pecking. Since fighting can lead to lower protein unit output due to increased stress, and even death, the industry has taken a fairly certain measure to put a stop to it: cutting off the birds' beaks. They used blowtorches in the past, but now the beaks of young chicks are inserted into guillotine-like devices with hot blades. There has even been serious talk of breeding blind chickens so they can't peck at each other. Despite these dramatic

FOR LOVE OF ANIMALS

measures, a certain amount of death is simply inevitable given the conditions in which these chickens are raised; it is built into the calculations of the business model. The primary goal is to maximize protein unit output per square foot of space, and this is consistent with even tens of millions of birds dying of various ailments before they get to slaughter.

Factory-farmed chickens have been bred to grow to their full size in only six weeks, at which point they are ready to be slaughtered. Workers grab birds by their legs (some industry welfare guidelines suggest that a reasonable limit is five birds per hand) and shove them into cages that are taken by truck to a slaughterhouse. Once there, the chickens have their feet snapped into metal shackles attached to a lightning-fast conveyer belt. Time is money, so the birds are killed at a rate of about one hundred per minute. But because the line is moving so fast it is inevitable that large numbers of chickens do not have their throats completely cut before they are dropped alive into a tank of scalding hot water.

The term *birdbrain* may have come from attempts to dismiss the moral status of chickens, but this would be a mistake. Anyone who has ever raised chickens knows that they are very social creatures, that they value their lives and those of their family members (especially their offspring), and know and respond to their own names. They even have morning and evening rituals. In short, much about their lives is morally significant.

Pigs

Pigs have a factory-farmed existence similar to that of chickens. However, because pigs are more sophisticated than chickens (they are actually very similar to dogs both in intelligence and their social lives), they suffer even more from the unending boredom.

This leads them to develop aggressive habits with other pigs, including frequent tail biting. For the same reason they debeak chickens, and undoubtedly causing a similar amount of pain, factory farmers solve this problem by simply cutting the tails off their pigs. Some of the worst treatment, however, is saved for pregnant sows; these hapless creatures are often moved to a farrowing pen in which an iron frame restricts almost all movement. They hate the pen so much that they will sometimes spend hours trying to chew through the iron bars. This may sound cruel, but these and other factory farm practices are all driven by the logic of profit and consumerism. Happily, farrowing pens have been essentially banned in most of Europe, and nine US states have also made them illegal. But the majority of American bacon, pork, and ham still come from pigs with mothers who didn't have the freedom even to simply turn around.

When selected for slaughter, pigs are generally crammed into a truck in which they are exposed to the elements. Some die of cold in the winter or of heat in the summer. Others die of suffocation in the tightly packed truck. Once pigs arrive in the slaughterhouse, workers attempt to stun them before their throats are cut on a conveyor belt; but as with chickens the rate of killing is so fast (over one thousand pigs every hour) that there are always those who have their throats cut while they are still conscious.

Factory-Farming Technology

There is far more than could be said about the practices of factory farms (please check out the suggestions for further reading for more information), but you now have at least a general sense of what is going on. These practices, because they run directly against the nature of these animals, have produced serious problems for the factory-farm business model. But like most modern people in the developed world, factory farmers have turned to technology for solutions. For instance, mostly because of American demand (particularly around Thanksgiving), factory-farmed turkeys are now bred to have breasts so large that they are no longer physically able to have sex. The solution to this significant problem has been documented everywhere from the TV show *Dirty Jobs* to special segments on National Public Radio. A male turkey must have his genitals manually stimulated by a factory farm worker to get his semen. This is affectionately called "securing the male's contribution." A hen must then be "broken" so that workers can insert a straw connected to the end of an air compressor and blast the semen into her.

But this might seem like yesterday's technology when compared to the sophisticated practices described by Dr. Yoav Eitan, the chief information officer of a major chicken breeding company in Israel. Eitan wants to demonstrate that his considerable computer skills are necessary for modern-day factory farms to maximize profit. He explains that factory farms breed chickens for several different characteristics—but because these characteristics sometimes conflict with each other, determining the exact combination of how each trait best relates to the other traits requires the analysis of powerful computer programs. These decisions are so delicate, and impact such a large number of animals, that profit margins can be dramatically affected by very small changes. Everything from slight differences in temperature and light intensity, for instance, can significantly affect protein unit output. But perhaps of most interest to us is what Eitan says in passing in his paper titled, "Information and Communication Technologies (ICT) Contribution to Broiler Breeding":

As a result of breeding for large and fast growing [chickens] with much better feed efficiency the modern [chickens] and their parents were genetically inclined towards uncontrolled eating, unchecked by the natural "feeling" of satiation. The destruction of satiation and feeding control mechanisms seriously affected laying ability, fertility and even the hatch percentage of fertile eggs.[5]

Let's be absolutely clear about what is being discussed in this quote. So that they will eat as much and as quickly as possible, factory farmed chickens have been genetically altered so that they are constantly hungry. Eitan and other factory farmers are worried about this, not because it is cruel to create billions of chickens who will never have the modest relief of a full stomach, but because these chickens are eating so much that (like the turkeys just mentioned) their size is impacting their ability to reproduce. This, of course, impacts the profit margins of the factory farm. With these kinds of attitudes and technologies, we are now light years from anything that resembles kindness and respect for animals. The logic of profit and consumerism has taken over completely.

Factory Farming and Human Beings

Factory farming not only harms tens of billions of nonhuman animals each year, but it seriously harms human beings as well. There is the moral harm (though difficult to calculate, it is no less real) done to the fabric of our culture when we support and participate in these violent structures of sin, of course. But let's get more concrete. Getting so many of our calories from factory farms has specific effects on human flourishing that we can clearly name and challenge.

For starters, factory farming is terrible for the environment in which many human beings live. These billions of nonhuman animals produce a tremendous amount of excrement: Such overwhelming quantities cannot be absorbed into the land. It gets into our drinking water system, and brings with it the antibiotics, hormones, pesticides, and heavy metals that factory farms put into the animals. Air quality around these farms is particularly terrible, and many local residents simply cannot bear to live within several miles—especially if they are downwind.

Those of you who have concerns about greenhouse gas emissions have (I hope) made lifestyle changes to lower your carbon footprint. Perhaps you have spent more money on cars with very high gas mileage or installed heating/cooling systems with this value in mind. Perhaps you have even limited your travel. These are praiseworthy lifestyle changes, especially from a Christian perspective on stewardship of the earth's resources. But the most serious way any of us contribute to greenhouse gas emissions is by supporting factory farms. Consider that livestock operations contribute 18 percent of all human-caused greenhouse gas emissions. This is more than the emissions of all the ships, planes, and automobiles—in the entire world—combined. In addition to the emissions from the huge uncovered lagoons of nonhuman animal excrement, huge amounts of methane, carbon dioxide, and nitrous oxide are produced by the digestive systems of the billions and billions of factory farmed animals.

But wait, there's more. The *Compendium of the Social Doctrine of the Church* insists that access to fresh water is a basic human right, but that right is under direct assault in many places and will soon be under assault in many more. The Central Intelligence

Agency is particularly worried that the future of international conflict will be organized around access to fresh water. We sometimes forget that only about 1 percent of the world's water is drinkable, and Americans use more water in one flush of the toilet than most people in the developing world use all day. What does this have to do with factory farming? Exact estimates vary, but it takes well over one thousand gallons of water to produce a single pound of beef. This means it takes over one million gallons of water to produce an average-sized steer. Do the math: In light of water scarcity alone, our support of institutions that farm these animals raises serious questions.

The production of calories this way is also wildly inefficient. Consider that it takes three units of fossil fuels to produce one "food energy unit" for all food products in the United States. But each food energy unit from meat produced in factory farms consumes over thirty units of fossil fuels. The most important reason for the difference is that we first need to grow crops to feed nonhuman animals in factory farms. These animals then use much of the energy from the crops to grow bones and other body parts that are not eaten. It would be dramatically more efficient simply to eat the crops in the first place rather than cycle them through the life of cow or pig and then eat only part of that animal.

Also consider the effect that factory farms have on the economic health of people living outside of urban areas. In 1950, 40 percent of people living in rural areas lived on farms. Today, that number is less than 10 percent. This change has devastated rural economies and, in some ways, destroyed an entire way of life. It is due in no small part to the effect that factory farming has had in putting smaller farms out of business. Just to name one piece of evidence, counties that have factory farms have higher rates of food stamp usage than similar counties without such farms. One could also point to higher poverty rates, lower wages for workers, and lower property values. Factory farming has led to meat becoming regularly available and affordable for those of us who live in cities, but this has come at a cost to rural communities. Indeed, contrary to common wisdom, a higher percentage of rural people live in poverty compared to city dwellers.

Finally, consider the issue of public health. As this book goes to press, the World Health Organization is monitoring a new and dangerous outbreak of bird flu in China and Taiwan—H7N9—a strain that has not previously been seen in human beings. It is likely just a matter of time before we have a bird flu pandemic which kills tens of thousands of people, if not more. And when this happens, we will almost certainly have the crowding of animals in factory farms to blame for the size of the outbreak. Many are also rightly worried about the creation of drug-resistant bacteria, and urge others to think about whether we actually need to take an antibiotic in any given situation. But consider that the number of antibiotics used by human beings is small when compared to the antibiotics poured into the bodies of tens of billions of nonhuman animals each year in factory farms. More than thirty million pounds of antibiotics are sold each year to be used on nonhuman animals, more than four times the number used on human beings. Unsurprisingly, a joint report from the Food and Drug Administration, the Agriculture Department, and the Centers for Disease Control and Prevention recently found that over half the meat samples they took from local supermarkets contained drug-resistant bacteria. Such bacteria almost always make it into the human community through workers in these farms. Many thousands of these workers, in addition to being at risk for acquiring this dangerous bacteria, often have other serious health problems, especially upper respiratory infections from the toxic gases and dust.

Let us conclude by thinking a bit more about workers in factory farms. What would drive someone to work in a place in which one has to constantly breathe in ammonia and expose oneself to drug-resistant bacteria? Where one has to "manually stimulate" the genitals of a turkey to get his semen? To grab chickens by the handful and shove them into cages? To shock, stun, and cut the throats of pigs by the thousands per day? To preside over conveyor belts and watch as chicken after chicken is killed in the timeliest way possible? To keep costs down, factory farm workers are not paid very well, and are not part of a union that protects their health and other interests. Indeed, it is probably not surprising to learn that most of the workers are poor, and many of them are undocumented immigrants or temporary foreign workers. These businesses need people who are far less likely to complain or quit in light of the horrific and damaging tasks they are required to complete.

Perhaps at this point we should recall Matthew Scully's admonition from the previous chapter. That we treat nonhuman animals this way is bad enough, but it is worse when we outsource that cruelty to someone else because we can't bear do it ourselves. Surely it is even worse—especially for followers of Christ—when the only ones who will do our dirty work are those who are poor and desperate for a source of income.

Questions for Discussion

1. In the first chapter we learned that Christians, and especially Catholics, should be sensitive to how consumerism and the search for profit affects vulnerable populations. How much should this concern be applied to factory farming?

2. Why do you think so few people are aware of what happens in factory farms? How has our culture become so disconnected from the process by which we get our food?

3. What is the best way to raise awareness about factory farms? What level of specificity is necessary to get people to understand what is happening in them? Does this chapter engage in the appropriate amount of specificity—without being emotionally manipulative?

4. What are some reasons that one could object to factory farms which go beyond the moral status and treatment of nonhuman animals?

Suggestions for Further Reading

Compendium of the Social Doctrine of the Church by the Pontifical Council for Justice and Peace

"Information and Communication Technologies (ICT) Contribution to Broiler Breeding" by Yoav Eitan[6]

Peter Singer and Christian Ethics by Charles C. Camosy

Putting Meat on the Table: Industrial Farm Production in America by the Pew Commission on Industrial Farm Animal Production

The Way We Eat: Why Our Food Choices Matter by Peter Singer and Jim Mason

CHAPTER EIGHT

EATING MEAT

IN SOME WAYS, EVERYTHING YOU have read so far leads up to these next two chapters. Too often academics and theologians like me write about things that, while sometimes interesting, matter very little to the actual lives of real people. Though I hope you have found the ideas in last seven chapters interesting on their own merits, the next two chapters will attempt to show that what we have read means dramatically changing how our lives affect nonhuman animals. Chapter nine will focus on animal research, hunting and pets, but this chapter will focus directly on our eating choices and habits.

This is an intimidating thought. For many of us, how we eat is deeply connected to our social lives and even family loyalties and memories. Certain dishes are eaten each year to celebrate holidays. Others have likely been passed down to us through the generations and can even make up part of our family identity. Others simply provide an important level of comfort and familiarity. However, these are all unacceptable reasons for participating in gravely unjust practices. Christians especially have a long and rich history of trying to conform our diets to the requirements of justice and holiness. Doing this in our secular, consumerist culture will not be easy, but if we are truly committed to a Christian life then our behavior will reflect our ideals. As Edmund Burke famously said: Conduct is the only language that rarely lies.

A Review of the Ideals

At this point it might help to review some ideals to which Christians are committed, especially as they touch on the topic of this chapter. Christians, of course, must start with the life of Jesus. And as we saw in chapter one, nothing was more central to his ministry than a concern for vulnerable populations on the margins—those "others" who were outside the circle of moral concern for the powerful. He was especially concerned when violence was the tool used to perpetuate their marginalization. And Jesus had particularly harsh words for those who let grasping for wealth and profit drive them to hurt vulnerable populations— suggesting that not only is the love of money the root of evil, but that those who act in these greedy ways will likely end up in hell. And it is not enough merely to avoid participating in violence and injustice but, at least if we want to avoid hell, we must actively seek to aid vulnerable populations who are so victimized.

The ancient world, of course, knew nothing of the monstrous and complex social structures we see in the developed West today. Catholic social teaching has attempted to apply Jesus's teachings about sin to, not merely a matter of an individual's choice, but involving systems and structures that are beyond the reach of any one person. Recall from chapter one that the *Compendium of the Social Doctrine of the Church* used the example of child labor abuses coming from the structure and logic of the unregulated free market. Instead of seeing children as full persons with inherent dignity, the logic of big business reduced them to a mere means of driving down labor costs and maximizing profit. Today, Catholic social teaching is still very much aware of how this plays out in a similar way in our modern social structures, but it gives special attention to the role that our American cultural focus on freedom, autonomy, and privacy plays in all of this. In many ways, this focus has led us away from describing the behavior of others as unjust and then pushing to change social structures so that this behavior is changed or even stopped.

Chapter one used the above insights to come up with the following definition of Christian justice:

> "CHRISTIAN JUSTICE MEANS CONSISTENTLY AND ACTIVELY WORKING TO SEE THAT INDIVIDUALS AND GROUPS—ESPECIALLY VULNERABLE POPULATION ON THE MARGINS—ARE GIVEN WHAT THEY ARE OWED. IT WILL BE ESPECIALLY SKEPTICAL OF PRACTICES WHICH PROMOTE VIOLENCE, CONSUMERISM, AND AUTONOMY."

Recall also the twin teachings of the *Catechism of the Catholic Church* about nonhuman animals. First, it claims that human beings owe them kindness. Second, we may only kill them or cause them to suffer in a situation of need.

Applying Christian Ideals to Factory Farms

As mentioned already, the overwhelming majority of meat that most of us eat—whether in a fast-food sandwich, on a plate at a four-star restaurant, or even in the stock of your homemade soup—comes from factory-farmed nonhuman animals. In light of the ideals just mentioned, how should Christians think about factory farms? I argue that factory farms are morally reprehensible institutions, particularly from a Christian perspective. If we care about justice, we Christians should not only refuse to support factory farms with our money, we should work to undermine the values and social structures that make it possible for them to function and flourish in the first place.

From the perspective of the Bible, our Christian tradition, and current Church teaching, nonhuman animals are cared for and valued by God independent of the interests of human beings. But it is precisely because most of us do not see nonhuman animals as objectively valuable—and have an important interest in seeing them as mere objects and products to satisfy our desires—that they are a vulnerable population which has been pushed to the margins of our culture and society. Those of us who follow the example of Jesus Christ, therefore, should give them special moral consideration and attention.

Christians should also be concerned about how the logic of violence and consumerism dominate the reasoning of factory farms. The attempt to maximize protein units per square foot is driven by both the customer's desire to buy meat at the cheapest possible price and the shareholder's desire to make a profit. This in turn drives factory farms to engage in practices that cause nonhuman animals horrific pain and suffering. Indeed, it has driven these farms even to push the boundaries of the species itself through artificial reproduction, breeding, and genetic manipulation. These practices didn't exist when small farms produced most of our meat, but the social structure of the market (especially when pushed by new cost-cutting technologies) forced the change. Given that our culture is dominated by the social structure of the market, the only way for a meat producer to stay in business is to drive down costs by factory farming.

And let's not forget the *Catechism*'s teaching that nonhuman animals are owed kindness. The treatment they receive in factory farms is about as far away from kindness as anyone could possibly imagine. To the extent that they care about the welfare of nonhuman animals, it is merely because it helps them get more protein units per square foot. As we saw in the previous chapter, these farms will treat their animals in the cruelest ways imaginable —and even risk dumping them by the millions (while still alive) into scalding hot water—if it will drive up profit margins.

Catholic teaching permits eating animals, but it also says that we may cause them to suffer or die only if we need to. Factory farms cause many billions of animals to suffer and die, that much is certain. The question then becomes, "Do we need to eat meat?" If you think carefully about why our culture eats meat, it is clear that we have two main reasons: (1) it is cheap and easy, and (2) it gives us pleasure. Neither comes close to the level of need. In fact, our decision to eat factory-farmed meat makes us a lot like Michael Vick running a dogfighting ring. He caused dogs to suffer and die for money and for pleasure. We eat factory-farmed animals for money and for pleasure. If we condemn Michael Vick, we likely condemn ourselves as well.

Are We *Really* Like Michael Vick?

So, eating meat is like running a dogfighting ring? Really? Surely some of you are thinking about important differences between the two. For instance, Michael Vick did terrible things to dogs, and aren't dogs different from other kinds of animals? This is surely true in the minds of most people in the developed West, but that perspective is really based on our culture rather than objective morality. In some households in Asia, for instance, they have precisely the opposite understanding of the relationship that we have between dogs and pigs. Pigs, rather than dogs, are the family pets. Indeed, in those cultures dogs are more likely to be used for food. It is understandable that some cultures have emotional attachments to certain animals, but the recent public controversy in Europe and the US about eating horsemeat shows that this emotional attachment cannot be justified. After all, why should we in the West care about eating horse versus eating pig versus eating dog? They are all very social, friendly, smart animals. There is virtually no difference, morally speaking, between torturing a dog to death and torturing a pig to death—especially when both are done in the interest of money and pleasure.

But perhaps there is another difference between our eating meat and what Michael Vick did. Vick was the ringleader, personally responsible for the torture and killing of dogs. Those of us who call up Domino's aren't actually torturing and killing the pigs who end up on our pizza, right? Don't we have several degrees of separation from the evil ways pigs are treated in factory farms? Unlike Vick's relationship with his dogs, these pigs are going to continue to be slaughtered and end up on top of billions of pizzas whether we choose to buy them or not.

These are important points to consider. Happily, John Berkman has thought about this topic quite a bit, and has applied the Catholic tradition's concept of "cooperation with evil" to our participation in factory farming. (The concept of cooperation with evil, incidentally, is becoming increasingly important in our globalized world as our participation in various evils becomes more complicated.

This rich Catholic idea deserves far more consideration.) Think about someone who, say, shows a terrorist how to make a suicide vest; if this person shares the aim of the terrorist, then this is what the Church would call "formal" cooperation with evil and it is going to be seriously wrong. But "material" cooperation is when a person clearly has a different aim and may not be morally guilty at all. Think of a pharmacist who unknowingly dispenses medication to a customer who uses it to poison someone else.

Given this framework, how should we think about someone who calls up Domino's and orders a pepperoni pizza? If we accept (as we should) that what was done in order to get the meat on the pizza was gravely evil, is the person who orders the pizza "formally" or "materially" cooperating with that evil? Berkman, writing in *A Faith Embracing All Creatures*, says that if this is material cooperation then the evil practices would have to be an unintended side effect that was not part of the shared aim of both the factory farm and the guy buying the pizza. But the guy wouldn't buy the pizza at all if he couldn't get it at the cheap price factory farming provides. And since the evil practices are what gets him this pizza at this price (meat from animals that are treated well is usually much more expensive), he does share the aim of the factory farm. He is formally cooperating with evil.

But suppose our pepperoni-lover claims that he really doesn't care about the few extra dollars the pizza might cost if it was ethical, and he just likes the taste and convenience of Domino's pizza delivery vs. the pizza he'd have to pick up at the Whole Foods two towns over. One could reasonably argue that this is material (and not formal) cooperation with evil. But even so, this doesn't let him off the ethical hook—at least from the perspective of Catholic teaching. For it to be morally acceptable material cooperation, where (unlike the pharmacist example above) you can foresee the evil with which you are cooperating, the Church says that the good gained must outweigh the evil produced. So let's compare: the good of the convenience and pleasure which the guy gets from getting a pizza delivered vs. the evil he supports in the torture and death of pigs in factory farms. I hope it goes without saying that this isn't a close call, and the evil produced far outweighs the good gained.

And don't forget there are other evils to consider in the comparison that go beyond what is done to nonhuman animals. Factory farms, remember, are responsible for more greenhouse gas emissions than all the cars, trucks, boats, planes, and jets in the world. They are responsible for the conditions that contribute to the development of drug-resistant bacteria and outbreaks of bird flu. They use fresh water and other scarce resources at wildly inefficient rates. They have devastated rural economies and ways of life. Don't forget that when we eat meat from factory farms we are also using the desperation of poor people—and often immigrants—to get them to do this dirty and unethical work for us. No, the balance sheet is clear: The cheapness of the price, the convenience of the store, and the pleasure of the taste do not outweigh the great evils perpetrated by our cooperation with factory farming. After all, our choice to buy their meat is the reason factory farms exist.

What about Health?

We might also wish to consider negative health effects when doing the comparison above. After all, in contributing to a culture of meat eating we perpetuate a social structure which systematically puts a lot of animal fat into our blood and even causes and fuels many different kinds of cancers. A 2012 study published in the *Archives of Internal Medicine* found, for instance, that each additional serving of red meat per day resulted in participants having a 13 percent higher chance of death during the study. And if it was processed red meat (such as hot dogs, bacon, or salami) that number jumped to 20 percent.

But the question of health could push in the other direction as well, particularly when we recall the *Catechism* talking about "need." After all, isn't a certain amount of meat necessary for human health? And what about those without the financial resources to get protein from free-range animals or from other sources? Aren't we condemning them to an unhealthy lifestyle? Maybe mere convenience or pleasure isn't enough to justify cooperating with the evil of factory farming, but what if that is the only way you can afford to keep yourself or your children healthy? Surely that rises to the level of need, doesn't it?

For starters, the need for very high levels of protein is greatly exaggerated in a society that is addicted to meat. For most of our history as a species, human beings have been practically vegetarian because meat was considered a luxury. We know that, for most adults, a well-balanced meatless diet will contain enough protein. It is sometimes true that children and pregnant women need more protein, but that can be supplied by eating more lentils, beans, and soy—cheap and plentiful sources of protein that challenge the idea that the poor need factory-farmed meat in order to be healthy. In fact, both the American Dietetic Association and the American Academy of Pediatrics claim that a meatless diet can be perfectly healthy for children, especially when the alternative makes them more likely to develop heart disease and cancer.

In *The Way We Eat* Jim Mason noted that vegetarians, on average, actually live longer than those who eat meat. Many different vegetarian cultures (especially in Asia and Central America) have longer life expectancies than those of us in the developed West. And even when we compare people who have similar lifestyles and environments, those who do not eat meat (like many Seventh Day Adventists) live longer than the general population. Mason also notes that vegan long-distance runner Scott Jurek recently shattered the ultrathon race record (135 miles in 115-degree heat) by a stunning thirty minutes. Another vegan, nine-time gold-medal-winner Carl Lewis, claimed that his best year of track competition was the year he stopped eating animals. National Football League stars Tony Gonzalez (the best tight end ever to play the game) and Arian Foster (the third-fastest NFL player ever to reach five thousand yards from scrimmage) are also among the high-performing athletes that have gone meatless. Vegan Fiona Oakes recently won a 2013 marathon—held at *the North Pole*. Needless to say, you can not only be perfectly healthy without eating meat, you can be one of the top athletes in the world.

I have tried to be fair in this chapter by highlighting some important considerations that challenge the animal-activist wisdom. However, you'll not be surprised when I say point-blank that I hope the majority of the facts and arguments I've presented convince you to give up factory-farmed meat. Remember in chapter four we read about the story from the Acts of the Apostles in which the early Christians were deciding how much of the Jewish Law to follow in their new religion? Remember that one of the practices they decided to keep was refusing to eat meat that had been sacrificed to idols? Perhaps today we hear this passage and simply say, "Well, nobody worships Jupiter anymore," and move on. But I submit that most of us are eating meat that has been sacrificed to idols—the false gods of consumerism and profit. The cruel suffering and death that is inflicted on many billions of nonhuman animals in factory farms every year is designed to drive the prices down so that (1) we can get our meat at a cheap price, and (2) the corporations which run factory farms can make a huge profit.

Like the early Christians, we should follow the biblical mandate to abstain from meat that has been sacrificed to our modern-day idols of consumerism and profit. We can and should strongly and publicly resist this practice in our personal eating decisions, and instead shop at places like Whole Foods, Trader Joe's, and local farms where we can be maximally sure that we are not participating in this social structure of sin. Christians should refuse to serve factory-farmed meat in their homes—even to guests who are expecting it. This would be a powerful witness to a Western world that is addicted to artificially cheap meat.

But when the issue is a matter of justice for vulnerable populations, our concern must go beyond our own practices. We must not allow "freedom" and "choice" to make space for grave injustice. Pastors of churches and bishops of dioceses should make sure that the institutions under their pastoral care refuse to serve factory-farmed meat. Catholic organizations and groups should be leading the way, particularly because we already have a framework of the *Catechism* and of cooperation with evil. All Christians should also work for social and structural change such that the law defends the God-given dignity and worth of all nonhuman animals as something far more than mere products in a market. This would mean, among other things, bringing these animals back to small family farms which respected this dignity, undermining the market's push to reduce their value simply to a means of profit.

Especially if you are thinking seriously about these issues for the first time, these changes may seem like a tall order. I know from personal experience how difficult they can be. I became convinced by these arguments at age twenty-four, but it took me six more years to make the commitment to give up meat (I figured that by thirty my practices had better start reflecting what I believe!), and now seven years later I still struggle especially when eating meat is connected to various family and holiday functions. But luckily for me, Christianity has a long tradition of fasting and spiritual discipline to help along the way. We have numerous examples of saints (especially the fathers of the desert) who show us how to imitate Christ's self-emptying, his rejection of sinful appetites, and—ultimately—his holiness. These people show us that God's Holy Spirit will give us spiritual food for the difficult journey away from factory-farmed food. All we need to do is ask.

QUESTIONS FOR DISCUSSION

1. Does giving up factory-farmed meat seem like a realistic proposition for you? Why or why not?

2. Do you think that there is a difference between eating free-range meat vs. factory-farmed meat? Why or why not?

3. Should we differentiate between eating various kinds of creatures? Is it worse to eat pigs than chickens? Worse to eat

chickens than fish? Does Jesus's eating fish impact your view?

4. How could Christian communities band together to support each other in their decisions to eat in ways that are biblically consistent and avoid injustice?

SUGGESTION FOR FURTHER READING

A Faith Embracing All Creatures edited by Andy Alexis-Baker and Tripp York

On Food and Cooking: The Science and Lore of the Kitchen by Harold McGee

The Vegetarian Solution: Your Answer to Cancer, Heart Disease, Global Warming, and More by Stewart Rose

The Way We Eat: Why Our Food Choices Matter by Peter Singer and Jim Mason

Why We Love Dogs, Eat Pigs and Wear Cows: An Introduction to Carnism by Melanie Joy

CHAPTER NINE

RESEARCH, HUNTING, AND PETS

In the previous chapter I was actually able to make a brief argument for a fairly definite position: It is wrong to participate in the gravely sinful social structure of factory farming. (For more detailed arguments please take a look at the suggestions for further reading.) In this chapter, however, I will avoid making this kind of argument and instead frame and ask some questions. Should we benefit from research on nonhuman animals? Should we hunt? Should we keep nonhuman animals as pets? I do not think there are obviously correct answers to these questions. For most of us, buying and eating meat from a factory farm is clearly sinful participation in injustice. But it is not clear that keeping pets, hunting, or buying drugs that have been tested on animals are in the same category. However, each of these actions raises moral questions about which most of us do not think very often, and what follows is my attempt to give you some good reasons to think very carefully about them.

Research on Nonhuman Animals

As with our discussion of factory farming, I refuse to bombard you with a series of emotionally manipulative stories. It would not be factually wrong to describe dogs being strangled (to study how their hearts are damaged) or pregnant baboons being purposely crashed on impact sleds (to study the violent impacts on their pregnancies). But such stories need context and a moral framework if we are going to investigate this issue in a way that is fair and respects the reader enough not to engage in raw emotional manipulation.

Background

In part because government oversight is spotty and uneven, we don't have very good estimates on the total number of nonhuman animals used in research. The best guesses I can find place it at around thirty million each year. In a nice summary of our current legal situation in a recent edition of *The Hastings Report*, Stephen Latham notes that our systems of regulation are complex and have many layers. Often, the left hand often does not know what the right hand is doing.

What he calls the "sprawling, strange, and often amended Animal Welfare Act of 1966" is the main law that regulates what laboratories can do to nonhuman animals. Its historical roots involve concern for pets and other popular animals (dogs, cats, rabbits, and monkeys), leaving many other kinds (including rats and mice) out of the sphere of concern, and virtually ignoring cold-blooded animals like the very intelligent octopus. When the law does choose to protect a nonhuman animal, it regulates standards of housing and pain control but not the scientific merit or promise of the experiment. Another kind of regulation comes from the National Institutes of Health (NIH) *Guide for the Care and Use of Laboratory Animals*. All labs that get federal funding most conform to the regulations in this document—and these cover warm- and cold-blooded creatures, including mice and rats. However, the guide is more about giving general standards (which are then open to wide interpretation), while the Animal Welfare Act institutes hard-and-fast rules.

Laboratory experiments are so numerous and varied that one can understand why the government relies on local "Institutional Animal Care and Use Committees" (IACUCs) to inspect and report on labs in their areas. However, these local IACUCs are not held publicly accountable—and, in part because they are made up of very different people, one committee could have a different standard than another. One IACUC might shut an experiment down, for instance, while another might let the very same experiment go. It is also problematic that these committees make no attempt to balance the medical importance of an experiment (or its chances for success) against harm done to nonhuman animals. This is a very important gap in regulation. Few people dispute that we may do *some* experimentation on nonhuman animals, but an important question is how much pain and suffering we may cause them relative to what kind of benefit we might get in return. Right now, this question isn't asked by our government regulators. It should be.

But some scientists would object to this kind of regulation. In other writings I have argued against the use of stem cell research that kills human embryos, and the response from some is that my position is "anti-science." Leaving aside the question of whether we need to destroy human embryos to get the best results from stem cell research (in my view, the record is overwhelmingly clear that we do not), it is not "anti-science" to discipline medical research with ethical principles and rules. In fact, one could argue the discipline of medical ethics was born out of the world's horrified reaction to Nazi medical research and attempts to make sure it would never happen again. It is actually *pro*-science to make it consistent with principles of justice and nonviolence. We must bring these concerns and values, not only to research done on human animals, but also those done on nonhuman animals.

Experiments on Nonhuman Persons?

Before exploring more about the "benefit vs. burden" of nonhuman animal research, let's pause and think about what made Nazi medicine so horrific. They got some "good" scientific results: Indeed, some of the data they developed about possible ways to treat hypothermia—achieved by forcing prisoners of war into vats of freezing cold water for hours at a time—has been sought after by scientists in our own time. But when we condemn this kind of experiment we don't do a "benefit vs. burden" calculation. Instead, we insist that the persons who were tortured and killed in these experiments are the kinds of being which have "irreducible moral worth." That is, their value is so high that it can't be fit into any "benefit vs. burden" calculation. For those (like the Nazis) who attempt to balance the harm of torturing and killing persons against the good of being able to treat other persons (pilots who were ditching into the ice cold North Sea), we say, "Persons are not the kinds of things that can be compared in this way." They have a value that cannot be reduced to this kind of calculation.

At first we might be tempted to say that only human beings could have this kind of value, and rule out nonhuman animals, but this would be too quick. Remember from chapter three that the Christian tradition makes a lot of room for *nonhuman* persons:

angels, aliens, giants, and so on. And don't forget Bilbo Baggins and Superman! So, no, one does not have to be *Homo sapiens* in order to be a person—but one must be a "substance of a rational nature." Are there nonhuman animals that might qualify?

Two reasonable candidates are primates and dolphins. A chimpanzee named Washoe, for instance, was able understand about 350 different signs from American Sign Language. She can even use many dozens of the signs herself to show that she is self-aware. When shown her reflection in a mirror and asked, "Who is that?" she replied: "Me, Washoe." She was even able to teach her adopted chimpanzee son to correctly communicate through signs.

Dolphins are arguably even more intelligent than are chimps, and they also demonstrate self-awareness by recognizing themselves in a mirror. We have also known for some time that dolphins have a complex system of communication, but we learned from a recent study published in *Proceedings of the Royal Society B* that they actually call each other by name: a unique whistle sound that refers to themselves or another dolphin. Interestingly, the study found that they seem to whistle with particular affection when calling the name of a family member or partner. At about the time this book went to press, someone sent me the viral YouTube video that caught a mother dolphin carrying the decaying body of her dead calf with her dorsal fin, and leading what many have called a funeral procession. Dolphins have now joined primates, human beings, and elephants among those animals we know understand death and mourn their dead.

This is impressive evidence of rationality. If what we mean by *person* is a being that is a substance of a rational nature, then it appears that great apes and dolphins (and other similarly intelligent nonhuman animals) are persons. And if they are persons, then they have irreducible moral value and should not be used in any kind of experiments at all. If this seems a remote fantasy that only an idealistic and out-of-touch professor could imagine, consider that Britain, New Zealand, and Spain have all had serious public discussion about granting limited human rights to primates. These would include the rights to life, liberty, and freedom from physical and psychological torture—and would also rule out almost all medical experiments.

Benefit vs. Burden

But not everyone is going to be convinced that primates and dolphins are in this category. Some have argued that—at least in the Christian tradition—being rational goes beyond self-awareness to the capacity to know and love God. Unfortunately, I don't have the space necessary to investigate what this might mean or if some nonhuman animals are capable of it. (If one believes, for instance, that atheist humans can know and love God by following God's voice in their conscience, then it would be interesting to explore recent studies which show that primates understand justice and other moral ideas.) But even if one rejects the idea that these nonhuman animals have irreducible value, clearly their value is nevertheless very high. It would take a significant benefit to justify causing them suffering and death.

Let me just propose some real-life scenarios to get us to think about how these benefit/burden calculations might play out. How should we think about the harm done to dolphins who are trained by the military to do, among other things, the dangerous (though obviously valuable) job of underwater mine detection? What about the attempts of psychologists to study the devastating effects of forced separation from parents and siblings on rhesus monkeys? Or how about attempting to study and cure Parkinson's by injecting primates with a drug which causes the disease? How should we go about weighing the benefit and burden in these situations? Remember that the burden on the nonhuman animal is not just from the experiment itself, but from having to spend most of its life in captivity: usually in a small cage. Remember also that the possible benefit is important and many millions of human beings around the world suffer and die from diseases like Parkinson's.

Some readers, perhaps uncomfortable with these calculations, might want us to move beyond monkeys at this point because they are so much like human beings and instead focus on animals that have less moral value. This is a bit of a Catch-22, given that the most certain benefit for humans comes from experiments on creatures that are most like us, but it is not always the case. Insulin is a virtual necessity in our diabetes-plagued developed world, and its invention saved the lives of many dozens of millions of people, but it was discovered by doing lab experiments on dogs. And today it is taken from the pancreases of slaughtered pigs.

And what about situations where we don't have this 20/20 hindsight? Right now we are crushing and cutting the spinal cords of cats in order to try to figure out how to treat back injuries in humans. Is that justified? Some feel that less "cute" animals, such as rats, have virtually no moral value, thus see no problem with doing almost any experiment on them—whether it is being slowly poisoned to death, given tumors, or purposely addicted to drugs. And though these experiments usually have some important benefit for humans, we should not underestimate the harm it does to the nonhuman animal. Rats have the same kind of nervous system as human beings and a new study in the journal *Science* found that, perhaps surprisingly, they show strong empathy for their fellow rats. Indeed, when presented with both options, the study found that rats prefer to free a trapped fellow rat than to feast on chocolate.

How do we do these benefit/burden calculations? I don't know that I have the answer to give you. A utilitarian approach—one which focuses purely on the greatest good for the greatest number—might try to argue that part of the benefit we should consider is the good things we develop from these experiments that could be used for the benefit of nonhuman animals as well in veterinary medicine. Some utilitarians would even say that many of these animals, because they were bred specifically for experimentation, are not harmed because they wouldn't even exist in the first place were it not for the experiments. Indeed, this kind of reasoning appears to justify similar experiments on human beings without their consent.

Utilitarians must wrestle with these complex philosophical problems, but Christians believe that both human and nonhuman animals have value that cannot be described in terms of a calculation. Each animal is cared for and loved by God, and God wills each animal's flourishing as the kind of thing that it is. Breeding animals for lives in cages, or seeing their value purely in terms of the benefit they can provide for others, misses this essential point. We Christians should remind ourselves of the *Catechism*'s wisdom here: We should only cause nonhuman animals to suffer and die if we need to. What this means is open to interpretation—and those who want justice for nonhuman animals should acknowledge the great need for medical research on animals—but having this idea in the front of our minds will frame the discussion in a more productive way.

Ways of Responding

Most of us are just as disconnected from the process by which we get drugs and other medical products as we are from how we get our food. Our consumerist culture, sadly, disconnects us from almost everything we buy. But just as with our food, we can ask questions about the source of our medical products and how they are produced. And perhaps using the model of cooperation with evil employed in the last chapter, we can make a decision about whether or not we should support certain kinds of laboratory experiments by buying the medical products they have produced.

But if we care about Christian justice for nonhuman animals, our duty cannot stop at this level. We must also engage in active, love-centered work for justice by raising awareness and pushing for change. Social pressure has already pushed laboratories to use more computer models to do things like toxicity tests, and the number of nonhuman animals used in laboratory experiments is going down. But we must keep the public pressure on so that more changes are implemented. Currently, regulatory agencies do not even weigh the burden on the animal against the (hoped-for) benefit of the experiment. Nor do they consider the inability of the nonhuman animal to flourish as the kind of thing that it is as part of the burden of the experiment. Both should change.

What would follow from these changes? While there would be new information to consider for the benefit/burden calculation, how the calculation would actually work is still not clear. This is true even if we say that the benefit must rise to the level of need. The most important thing to do, at least at this early stage, is simply to have a national conversation and then start to craft public policy that reflects any national consensus. This has happened outside the United States already—particularly in connection with experiments on great apes and monkeys—but it is starting to happen in this country as well. NIH support for experimenting on chimps, for instance, has been halted and there are growing calls to stop all such invasive research on all primates. Christians should be among the most energetic leaders in our coming national conversation about nonhuman animal research.

Hunting

I grew up in rural Wisconsin. Many of my friends and some of my family are hunters. Places like our local bar and grill would simply shut down during hunting season—after all, so many people were out hunting that it made little sense to stay open. My personal experience of hunters leads me to see them in a different category from that of factory farmers. For starters, they are far more connected to the process by which a nonhuman animal is killed. Especially if they are killing in order to eat the animal—or to thin the population for its own good—they do not outsource the job to someone else. They have the courage and skill to do it themselves. Many of them have a deep respect for nature and the animals they kill, and will sometimes do things that border on rituals to honor their beauty and goodness of their lives. This is a far cry from seeing them purely as protein products from which one can make profit. Indeed, sometimes the meat procured from a hunt is donated to food banks that serve the poor.

But we should not have a naïvely positive view of hunters. When we break it down, they are still causing nonhuman animals to suffer and die for pleasure. The main reasons hunters hunt (rather than just take a walk in the woods) include the thrill of the hunt and the kill, the social time—and, let's be honest, showing off and competing—with their buddies, creating trophies to hang in their homes, and even developing skill sets like following a blood trail. One particular hunter's blog urges those who do not kill with one shot to follow blood trails and finish off the nonhuman animals they have wounded. Failure to do so, the blog says, gives "dangerous ammunition to the arsenal of anti-hunting groups." Indeed. All one needs to do is think of a wounded animal bounding away from his attacker in horror, searing pain, and abject fear to begin to question whether hunting is justified. To get a sense of the kinds of wounds with which the nonhuman animal may be suffering, consider the blog's very detailed advice for following the blood trail:

> Examine the arrow for blood or other signs of where it might have traveled through the animal. Check the ground for hair or blood that can aid you in determining where the animal was hit. If you hit the deer in the liver, there will be brown hair and thick, dark blood left behind. If it was hit in the lungs or heart, there will be brown hair and a lighter colored blood there. If you hit it in the stomach, there will be white hair, watery blood and green-colored stomach contents.[7]

And while it is certainly true that some hunters are more in tune with nature and the relationship that has existed between human and nonhuman animals for thousands of years, hunting has become increasingly infected with technology and consumerism. A simple search on Amazon.com produces dozens of "fawn distress" devices that can lure prey within shooting range of human predators. Or type in "hunting heat sensor" and you'll find any number of gadgets designed to find and kill nonhuman animals based on tracking their body heat. Or how about high-tech devices used to detect nonhuman animals in your blind spots? While perhaps making humans more effective killers of animals, this move toward technology-driven hunting is hardly in tune with nature in the way we sometimes imagine hunting to be.

Once again we return to the teaching of the *Catechism*: It is wrong to needlessly cause nonhuman animals to suffer and die. For most kinds of hunting, except perhaps for the very few who need the food to live or be healthy, the suffering and death that is caused hardly rises to the level of "need." But my hunter-friendly friends do have a powerful objection left to them. Isn't it the case that many kinds of animals will suffer and die unless we hunt them? Perhaps, due to lack of predators, there are too many animals relative to the food sources available. Many such animals will starve to death. Perhaps, due to the expansion of the habitat of human animals, nonhuman animals in these areas are likely to get hit by cars or other vehicles. Such animals will likely die a slow death on the side of the road. Isn't it better that they are killed by hunters and that the meat be donated to food banks? This is an important objection and, to be honest, I think it makes it difficult to condemn *all* kinds of hunting.

Hard-core opponents of hunting could respond by saying, "Well, the reason they have no predators is because human beings have killed all of them." But is it really better for them to be mauled to death by a wolf than shot by a hunter? Hunting opponents could also note that sprawling human settlements—driven by a consumerist and peculiarly American desire to be "independent" and "free" in a large home and yard—are what drive many nonhuman animals to be killed by cars and other vehicles. That's true, and there are multiple reasons to challenge the American assumption that our goal should be to live independently on a large estate, but what should we do in the meantime? Continue to let thousands of animals be slaughtered by huge chunks of metal flying by at sixty miles per hour?

These are not easy questions and, once again, I do not mean to answer them for you in this chapter. There do seem to be some circumstances in which hunting nonhuman animals is consistent with respect for such animals—apart from the pleasure humans get from hunting them. If we do need to hunt some nonhuman animals for their own good, however, we may want to question whether hungover weekend warriors (who, again, are mainly out there to socialize) are the best candidates for the job. Perhaps counties and townships should instead hire expert marksmen so that the animals killed have the best chance of dying without suffering. At any rate, these are complicated questions which I simply want to frame for you, the reader, to carefully consider.

Pets

Most people reading this book will have owned a pet at one point in their lives. Perhaps that pet even played a central role in your happiness and well-being. I know that the sheepdog with which I grew up, Clancy, played this role in my own life. But because Clancy was an "outside dog" we subjected him to the elements in ways that would have been unthinkable for human beings. Though we did some things to try to keep him warm, he endured many ridiculously cold Wisconsin winters, and many hot and humid summers. In his old age he became so frightened of thunderstorms that he destroyed several teeth while trying to chew his way through the garage door. It still makes me sad and sick to my stomach to think about this.

But inside pets have their own problems. While outside dogs can flourish more as the kinds of things they are by having room to run free and explore open spaces and fresh air, inside dogs cannot express this nature and often become cramped, depressed, and antisocial. Far too often they spend most of their miserable days in small cages or crates, and are forced to hold their bladders and bowels for an unreasonable and painful length of time. Boredom and lack of exercise are also serious problems for these dogs. These inside pets are kept from flourishing as the kinds of animals they were meant to be.

Consumerism and the market for pets create ethical problems as well. In part because we think of our pets as objects that we own, we expect quality control over these products. Many of us, perhaps driven by popular culture or social status, want to own dogs that are purebred. But this is problematic on several levels. First, the characteristics for which certain animals are bred are often not good for the animals themselves. The flat faces, for instance, of certain breeds of dogs make it difficult for them to exercise—or even breathe normally. But just as importantly, the obsession that many of us have with pure breeds means that breeders will manufacture the products we want in puppy mills—which are akin to factory farms when it comes to their horrific conditions. Many pets are available in animal shelters, just waiting for someone to adopt them, but our obsession with purity and turning nonhuman animals into products to fulfill our desires means that millions of these animals are euthanized instead of adopted.

Some would say that we should not own nonhuman animals in the first place. After all, doesn't their intrinsic value mean that, unlike objects or products, they aren't the kinds of things we can own? Furthermore, owning a pet risks putting us in the dangerous consumerist mind-set. With the advent of doggie strollers, cat clothes, and gourmet pet food, we can lose our sense of duty toward vulnerable and poor populations almost as easily as when we spend unnecessary resources on human beings.

However, when we recall our discussion of Genesis 2, it does seem clear that God intended human and nonhuman animals to be companions. One of the best ways children and other human beings can learn this theological truth is to have regular social interaction with other animals. In fact, it may be our experience with pets that grounds our respect for other animals more generally. Some criticize zoos for reasons similar to those used by those who criticize pet ownership, and in certain circumstances there is good reason to push for reform, but they, too, allow us to experience the wonder and majesty of God's creatures up close. These experiences can and often do lead to an appreciation for their value and moral treatment.

Should you use drugs from a clinical trial that was cruel to animals? What about going on a hunting trip with your friends? Is it a good idea to check out adoption day at PetCo? Without knowing more about your circumstances, I can't answer these questions. But I hope I've framed them for you in the context of some of the ethical commitments already explored in this book. When Christians think about how to answer these questions, we must do so in light of our values of justice and nonviolence; of our understanding that animals are "good" independent of how they can serve our interests; and our commitment to refusing to cause animals suffering or death without need. The questions posed in this chapter are not easy ones, and the answers to which we are led may force us to change our lives in significant and even uncomfortable ways. But fear of this, while understandable, is an unacceptable reason for failing to wrestle with these important questions.

QUESTIONS FOR DISCUSSION

1. Are animals like chimps and dolphins persons? Should we ever use rational and self-aware animals for research?
2. Should we ever use dogs and cats for medical research? What kind of research? How much pain and suffering is acceptable? Do you think differently about using pigs or rats? Why or why not?
3. Why do people hunt? Do they need the meat? Is it mostly for fun? Does it rise to the level of "need" insisted upon by the *Catechism of the Catholic Church*?
4. Is it important to "thin the herd" of certain kinds of animals? If yes, who should do it? Everyday hunters? Expert marksmen? Others?
5. Is it acceptable to own pets if they are trapped in a cage or tied up outside for most of the day? Should humans be able to buy and own nonhuman animals?

SUGGESTIONS FOR FURTHER READING
Animal Research Ethics from the Hasting Center Report
Dominion by Matthew Scully
"Following Blood Trails & Finding Every Buck" by Bob Foulkrod[8]

"HR 13881: The Animal Welfare Act of 1966" by the United States House of Representatives

God, Humans, and Animals: An Invitation to Enlarge Our Moral Universe by Robert N. Wennberg

Guide for the Care and Use of Laboratory Animals by the National Institutes of Health

In the Company of Animals: A Study of Human-Animal Relationships by James Serpell

Peter Singer and Christian Ethics by Charles C. Camosy

"Vocal Copying of Individually Distinctive Signature Whistles in Bottlenose Dolphins" by Stephanie L. King, et al.

Wild Justice: The Moral Lives of Animals by Marc Bekoff and Jessica Pierce

Why Animal Suffering Matters by Andrew Linzey

CHAPTER TEN

A CONSISTENT ETHIC OF LIFE

MOST EVERYONE READING THIS BOOK has a principle in which you believe very strongly. Here's a common one: "All human beings deserve equal protection of the law." But applying a principle like this, as an old philosophy professor of mine used to say, is like riding a bus—and *not* like taking a taxi. By this he meant that, like riding a bus, applying a principle means you are forced to follow it wherever it goes. Unlike taking a taxi, you don't get to tell your own principles where they end up. So, for instance, say your principle leads you to conclude that Catholics and Protestants should have equal protection of the law. You must then ride the bus to saying whites and blacks, men and women, heterosexuals and non-heterosexuals, prenatal children and infants—and every other member of the human species—also has equal protection of the law. Some of these other conclusions, perhaps due to your political commitments, may be difficult to accept. But that's just too bad. You are obligated to suck it up and consistently follow your principle wherever it leads you.

If you find yourself unable to consistently apply a principle, then perhaps you need to ask yourself honestly whether you actually believe it is true. Perhaps it is time to get on a different bus and take a new path. That is a perfectly acceptable and even noble response when one is confronted with inconsistency. What is not acceptable, however, is pretending that having a principle is like taking a taxi. You don't get to tell your principles when they apply and when they don't. You don't get to allow self-deception, willful ignorance, or anything else keep you from consistently applying your principles. As we saw in chapter one, this kind of inconsistency allows radical injustice to flourish and hurts many vulnerable populations. Inconsistent application of the principle of equal protection of the law, for instance, is what allows for unjust discrimination against nonwhites, females, and prenatal children. This cannot and should not stand. Everyone, especially Christians, should not only be trying to eradicate discrimination against these vulnerable populations in our own lives, but also be standing up publicly and demanding consistent application of the principle that all human beings deserve equal protection of the law. Justice demands consistency.

Throughout this book I have attempted to show that, especially from a Christian perspective, our culture refuses to apply its principles consistently when it comes to the moral status and treatment of nonhuman animals. This has produced a set of radical injustices that are as predictable as they are horrible. I have called everyone, but especially Christians, to avoid speciesism and follow our principles consistently as they apply to nonhuman animals.

Consistent Application of Our Principles

Let's do a quick review of our most important principles and how they might apply to questions about how we should treat nonhuman animals:

Imitating the love of Jesus means behaving in nonviolent ways.

Imitating the love of Jesus means having a preference for the most vulnerable.

Imitating the love of Jesus means resisting the love of money, profit, and consumerism.

Human beings are called to be good stewards of God's creation and to care for it with Jesus as our primary example of what good stewardship means.

All creation is created good by God independent of the interests of human beings.

Nonhuman animals are created by God to be our companions, not our food.

"Need" is the only thing that justifies causing animals to suffer and die.

Some of you may reject one or more of these principles, and thus will be riding a different kind of bus. But for Christians, and especially for Catholic Christians, these principles reflect the most important sources of moral truth in our tradition. It will not be easy to lay them aside without laying Christianity aside as well. And perhaps this leads us to another question that my readers will need to ask themselves honestly: When it comes right down to it, do the truths of the Christian tradition trump other values and concerns in our lives—or is it the other way around? Perhaps some of us need to ask whether we are on a Christian bus at all. Perhaps we don't want to be. Whether we are talking about issues surrounding nonhuman animals, or another set of issues, the Christian bus isn't an easy ride.

But if we truly are committed to these principles, then we need to take an honest and deep look inside ourselves and ask what this looks like in real life. Is factory farming consistent with our principles? Should we support factory farms by purchasing their meat? What about eating animal products (eggs, cheese, milk) from these farms? Is eating animals that are treated well and painlessly killed in a different category? What kinds of research on animals are acceptable and which are not? Should we support and benefit from unethical research? Should we hunt? Should we even own pets?

For many of us, merely thinking seriously about giving honest answers to these questions can be deeply disturbing. Many of our traditions, social structures, routines, and even relationships would likely be significantly affected (or even destroyed) if we consistently applied our principles. This reveals just how deeply dependent our culture has become on unjust and violent treatment of nonhuman animals. It is also a classic example of why Christians are called to stand up for vulnerable populations; their dignity is often simply too inconvenient for the powerful to recognize and respect. Therefore, our job as individual Christians is not only to passively refuse to be part of the powerful group which refuses to acknowledge the dignity of the vulnerable group, but also to imitate Christ's love and actively work to change social structures and laws so that these populations are given a voice.

The Role of the Church Community

What I'm proposing in this book will likely seem so difficult precisely because our culture expects and supports practices and values of us which seem to require unjust treatment of nonhuman animals. But here is a tailor-made opportunity for the Church to be the Church. We can begin to create just structures of community which resist the unjust structures in our broader culture.

Christians, for instance, should expect to come to Church events and not be served factory-farmed meat. Churches should work to make just and ethical forms of food available to the community—perhaps by helping to connect parishioners to the sources of their food. Churches could help make their congregations aware of farmers in the community who produce and sell ethical food. Perhaps they could even have ethical food available from farmers' markets organized on Church property. Perhaps the social justice and pro-life parish committees could work together and have regular discussions and workshops on how to eat and live in just relationship with nonhuman animals. Even just having a strong community of people, knowing that we are all struggling to consistently apply our common principles on these issues, would make the burden easier to bear. Isn't this struggle as a Church community part of what Lent is supposed to be about? Perhaps Catholics could return to our more rigorous fasting traditions and ask practicing Catholics to avoid meat during all of Lent and on every Friday outside of Lent.

But as Pope Francis has emphasized, we cannot limit ourselves to being a self-referential Church. Like Jesus, we must go out and preach the Gospel of love and nonviolence outside our church communities. Though we have by no means been perfect on this score, Christianity has often been a public leader when it comes to liberation and justice movements: from Martin Luther King, Jr., fighting for racial equality to Mother Teresa working for the poor in India to Pope John Paul II insisting on justice for our prenatal children. To this proud history the Christian churches should now add a very public and intense fight for the liberation of nonhuman animals. Evangelicals like William Wilberforce and Catholics like

Mary Ebertstadt serve as models for us in this regard. Not only is commitment to other human causes like racial equality and the pro-life movement not a reason to avoid the animal liberation movement, it is a reason to join it. The Church must and should lead on this new issue of liberation. It is what we do.

Far too often, our political commitments hide more truth than they reveal. If you think of yourself as a conservative Christian, you may have picked up this book and assumed from its cover and subject matter that you could dismiss it as soft, sentimental, and perhaps even lacking in serious Christian commitment. But if you did a fair reading, you soon came to realize that none of those labels apply. Authentic Christian commitment transcends the inadequate liberal/conservative binary categories of our secular political culture. True Christians are ruled by our relationship with Jesus. What this relationship demands of us cannot possibly be made to fit into the categories of secular American politics. Indeed, we should be skeptical of those who call themselves Christians but fit neatly into secular political categories. Most likely they have secular politics—and not their relationship with Jesus Christ—as the most important thing in their lives.

Justice for nonhuman animals is something about which both liberal and conservative (if we must use these problematic labels) Christians should be able to agree. And this is true not only when it comes to the issues that directly impact animals, but also the other effects on humans: ecological devastation, economic inefficiency, destruction of rural community, heart disease and cancer, drug resistant bacteria and bird flu, hiring and treatment of immigrant workers, and so on. We should apply the above principles consistently to nonhuman animals, not only because justice for these creatures requires it, but also because they are connected to so many other kinds of issues as well. If we get on board the Christian bus, we will find ourselves on a ride forcing us to consider many different kinds of interconnected topics. A consistent ethic of life demands no less.

If anyone needed proof that sin has screwed up our world on a massive scale, all we need to do is ask them look at the horrific and cruel injustices perpetuated upon nonhuman animals. But as Christians we know that Jesus has redeemed human beings and all of creation. This redemption has already happened, but it has not been fully implemented. More work remains. In giving human beings dominion over creation, God has charged each of us with protecting its many creatures—both human and nonhuman.

How will we respond?

QUESTIONS FOR DISCUSSION

1. Do you believe that Christian principles should always trump other goods and concerns in your life? If not, what does it mean to call oneself a Christian? When would God's principles be trumped by our own desires or the desires of someone other than God?

2. Why do you think so few people consistently apply their principles when it comes to treatment of nonhuman animals?

3. What responsibility do you think you have to change your life when it comes to just treatment of nonhuman animals? Do you have a responsibility to make sure that justice for nonhuman animals exists in the law and other social structures as well?

4. Sometimes concern for nonhuman animals is labeled a "liberal" idea and conservatives reject it on that basis alone. Do you think Christians should have primary allegiance to our theological principles or our political ones?

SUGGESTIONS FOR FUTURE READING

A Community of Character: Toward a Constructive Christian Social Ethic by Stanley Hauerwas

Consistent Ethic of Life by Joseph Cardinal Bernardin

The Consistent Ethic of Life: Assessing its Reception and Relevance edited by Thomas A. Nairin

Consistently Opposing Killing: From Abortion to Assisted Suicide, the Death Penalty, and War, edited by Rachel MacNair and Stephen Zunes

Green Discipleship: Catholic Theological Ethics and the Environment edited by Tobias Winwright

NOTES

1. Available at http://www.vatican.va/holy_father/
   john_paul_ii/messages/peace/documents/
   hf_jp-ii_mes_19891208_xxiii-world-day-for-peace_en.html.
2. Citing *Centesimus Annus,* 37–38, referencing Matthew 6:26;
   Daniel 3:79–81; Genesis 2:19–20; 9:1–4.
3. Quoted at http://www.animalliberationfront.com/Practical/
   Shop—ToDo/Religion/PopeBenedictXVI.htm.
4. *Sollicitudo Rei Socialis,* 34, http://www.vatican.va/
   holy_father/john_paul_ii/encyclicals/documents/hf_jp-ii_
   enc_30121987_sollicitudo-rei-socialis_en.html, accessed
   June 24, 2013.
5. Quoted at http://departments.agri.huji.ac.il/economics/
   breeding-yoav-2012.pdf.
6. Quoted at http://departments.agri.huji.ac.il/economics/
   breeding-yoav-2012.pdf, accessed March 5, 2013.
7. "Following Blood Trails & Finding Every Buck," at
   BobVoukrod.com, http://www.bobfoulkrod.com/?page_
   id=913, accessed June 24, 2013.
8. "Following Blood Trails & Finding Every Buck," at
   BobVoukrod.com, http://www.bobfoulkrod.com/?page_
   id=913, accessed June 24, 2013.

ABOUT THE AUTHOR

Charles C. Camosy is an assistant professor of Christian ethics at Fordham University. He is the founder and co-director of the Catholic Conversation Project and the author of *Peter Singer and Christian Ethics: Beyond Polarization*. He holds a B.A., M.A., and Ph.D. from the University of Notre Dame.